Japan Today and How It Got This Way

James M. Vardaman
Aiba Tae = translator

日本の論点
（にほん　ろんてん）

ジェームス・M・バーダマン
相場 妙 = 訳
（あいば　たえ　やく）

Furigana JAPAN
日本の論点
Japan Today and How It Got This Way

© 2014 James M. Vardaman
© 2017 IBC Publishing, Inc.

Published by IBC Publishing, Inc.
Ryoshu Kagurazaka Bldg. 9F, 29-3 Nakazato-cho
Shinjuku-ku, Tokyo 162-0804, Japan

www.ibcpub.co.jp

All rights reserved. No part of this book may be reproduced in
any form without written permission from the publisher.

First edition 2017

ISBN978-4-7946-0465-1

Printed in Japan

About *Furigana JAPAN*

Reading Sets You Free

The difficulty of reading Japanese is perhaps the greatest obstacle to the speedy mastery of the language. A highly motivated English speaker who wants to make rapid progress in a major European language such as Spanish, French or German need only acquire a grasp of the grammar and a smattering of vocabulary to become able to at least attempt to read a book. Thanks to a common alphabet, they can instantly identify every word on the page, locate them in a dictionary, and figure out—more or less—what is going on.

With Japanese, however, *kanji* ideograms make it infinitely harder to make the jump from reading with guidance from a teacher to reading freely by oneself. The chasm dividing the short example sentences of textbooks from the more intellectually rewarding world of real-world books and articles can appear unbridgeable. Japanese—to borrow Nassim Taleb's phrase—is an "Extremistan" language. *Either* you master two thousand *kanji* characters with their various readings to achieve breakthrough reading proficiency and the capacity for self-study *or* you fail to memorize enough *kanji*, your morale collapses, and you retire, tired of floating in a limbo of semi-literacy. At a certain point, Japanese is all or nothing, win or lose, put up or shut up.

The benefits of staying the course and acquiring the ability to read independently are, of course, enormous.

Firstly, acquiring the ability to study by yourself without needing a teacher increases the absolute number of hours that you can study from "classroom time only" to "as long as you want." If there is any truth to the theories about 10,000 hours of practise being needed to master any skill, then clearly the ability to log more hours of Japanese self-study has got to be a major competitive advantage.

Secondly, exposure to longer texts means that your Japanese

3

input rises in simple quantitative terms. More Japanese *going into* your head means that, necessarily, more Japanese *stays in* your head! As well as retaining more words and idioms, you will also start to develop greater mental stamina. You will get accustomed to digesting Japanese in real-life "adult" portions rather than the child-sized portions you were used to in the classroom.

Thirdly, reading will help you develop tolerance for complexity as you start using context to help you figure things out for yourself. When reading a book, the process goes something like this: You read a sentence; should you fail to understand it first time, you read it again. Should it still not make sense to you, you can go onto the next sentence and use the meaning of that one to "reverse-engineer" the meaning of its predecessor, and so on. By doing this, you will become self-reliant, pragmatic and—this is significant—able to put up with gaps in your understanding without panicking, because you know they are only temporary. You will morph into a woodsman of language, able to live off the land, however it may be.

That is the main purpose of *Furigana JAPAN*: to propel you across the chasm that separates those who read Japanese from those who cannot.

Furigana the Equalizer

Bilingual books have been popular in Japan since the 1990s. Over time, they have grown more sophisticated, adding features like comprehensive page-by-page glossaries, illustrations and online audio. What makes the *Furigana JAPAN* series—a relative latecomer to the scene—special?

The clue is in the name. This is the first ever series of bilingual books to include *furigana* superscript above every single *kanji* word in the text. Commonly used in children's books in Japan, *furigana* is a tried-and-tested, non-intrusive and efficient way to learn to read *kanji* ideograms. By enabling you to decipher every word immediately, *furigana* helps you grasp the meaning of whole passages faster without needing to get bogged down in fruitless and demoralizing searches for the pronunciation of individual words.

By providing you with the pronunciation, *furigana* also enables you to commit new words to memory right away (since we remember more by sound than by appearance), as well as giving you the wherewithal to look them up, should you want to go beyond the single usage example on the facing English page. *Furigana JAPAN* provides a mini-glossary at the foot of each page to help you identify and commit to memory the most important words and phrases.

Raw Materials for Conversation

So much for *furigana*—now for the "Japan" part of the name. The books in this series are all about Japan, from its customs, traditions and cuisine to its history, politics and economy. Providing essential insights into what makes the Japanese and their society tick, every book can help you as you transition from ignorant outsider to informed insider. The information the books contain gives you a treasure trove of raw materials you can use in conversations with Japanese people. Whether you want to amaze your interlocutors with your knowledge of Japanese religion, impress your work colleagues with your mastery of party-seating etiquette and correct bowing angles, or enjoy a heated discussion of the relative merits of arranged marriages versus love marriages, *Furigana JAPAN* is very much the gift that keeps on giving.

We are confident that this series will help everyone—from students to businesspeople and diplomats to tourists—start reading Japanese painlessly while also learning about Japanese culture. Enjoy!

Tom Christian
Editor-in-Chief
Furigana JAPAN Series

はじめに

「日常的な場面なら、だいたいは意志疎通を図ることができた。でも、今の日本で起きていることをあれこれ聞かれたときには、答えられなかった」——海外から帰国した日本人の感想で、これほど嘆かわしいものはそうあるものではない。

グローバル化の必要性が日本でこれだけ論じられているにもかかわらず、全般的に日本人が自分の国に関する会話に積極的に参加できていないことは残念なことである。それらは外国の大人たちが知りたいと思っている出来事なのである。あなたは彼らの世界を知りたいし、彼らはあなたの世界が知りたい。これは、膝を突き合わせてのコミュニケーションなら当然ながらお互い思うことであり、双方にとって有意義な会話の中身となるはずである。

日本人は、話題に上る問題について理解こそしているかもしれないが、外国の人々に英語でどう説明するかは考えていないことが多い。この本が多少なりともこの状況に変化をもたらしてくれることに期待したい。本書は今後しばらくは重要となるであろう現代の話題を幅広く網羅している。今日問題となっていることについて何かしらの理解を促してくれるであろうし、どの項目についてもわずかながら背景となるような情報を載せている。

Preface

There are few sadder comments made by Japanese who return from abroad than "I was usually able to communicate in everyday situations. But I was asked many questions about what is happening in Japan today, and I wasn't able to respond."

Despite all of the talk in Japan about the need for "globalization," it is unfortunate that in general Japanese are unable to actively participate in conversations about their own country. These are the kinds of topics that adults from other countries are interested in learning about. You want to learn about their world; they want to learn about yours. This is a natural part of sharing in face-to-face communication, and it can be very rewarding to both parties in the conversation.

Japanese may understand the issues that are brought up, but often they have not considered how to explain those issues in English to people from other countries. This book hopes to change that, in some small way. It covers a broad range of the main contemporary subjects that will continue to be important in the coming years. Where it may be helpful in understanding something that is an issue today, each item provides a small amount of background information.

本書はまず、特に国際関係の観点から見て日本全体に関わる問題を取り上げている。その後に政治、経済、社会、日々の暮らし、原子力、文化などの話題が続く。領土問題、放射能除染、職場における男女平等といった深刻な話題から、旨味、老舗、自動販売機といった比較的軽い話題まで、さまざまな会話の場面に対応できるような配分を考えた。

　日本語と英語の対訳形式なら、読者はわからない単語をいちいち調べなくても日本語を読むことができる。英語版が助けてくれるからである。ただし対訳が必ずしも一語一句対応の逐語訳でないことはご留意いただきたい。この本の目的は、訳例となることではなく、読者が必要な日本語の語彙や表現を学ぶ際の一助となることである。

　日本には世界に提供できるものがたくさんあるが、実際に提供するためには他者との意志疎通が欠かせない。日本語でそれをするにはどうしたらよいか、つまり日本人が使うツールで意志疎通を図るにはどうしたらよいか、本書が読者の考察を促すことを願っている。

ジェームス・M・バーダマン

The volume begins with issues that involve Japan in general, especially in terms of international relations. Following that are sections including topics from politics, economics, society, daily life, nuclear power, culture, education and the recovery of the Tohoku region. Items range from serious topics like territorial disputes, nuclear decontamination, and workplace gender equality to lighter topics such as *umami*, *shinise* and vending machines. We have tried to balance subjects to prepare for a variety of conversational situations.

The Japanese-English *taiyaku* format allows the reader to read the Japanese without looking up each unknown word. The English version conveys that information. Please note that *taiyaku* does not necessarily mean word-for-word translation. The purpose of this book is to provide help the reader learn the necessary Japanese vocabulary and wording, not to serve as a model for translation.

Japan has a lot to offer the world, and to do that, it is necessary to communicate with other people. It is our hope that this volume will help the reader consider how to do that in Japanese, a tool that is used by the Japanese.

James M. Vardaman

目次

はじめに 6
Preface 7

国家 *The Nation* 15

憲法改正 16
Revision of the Constitution 17

靖国神社問題 22
Yasukuni Shrine issue 23

米軍基地 26
American bases 27

皇位継承 30
Imperial succession 31

食料自給率 34
Food self-sufficiency rate 35

かっこいい日本 38
"Cool Japan" 39

日本の「幸福度ランキング」 42
Japan's "Happiness Rank" 43

政治 Politics 45

領土問題 46
Disputed territories 47

謝罪と戦争責任 50
Apologies and war responsibility 51

経済 Economics 55

年金危機 56
National pension crisis 57

働く女性 60
Women in the workforce 61

築地移転 64
Moving Tsukiji 65

老舗 68
Shinise, long-established enterprises 69

社会 Society 73

人口高齢化 74
Graying of the population 75

人口減少 78
Shrinking population 79

格差社会 *84*
かくさしゃかい
Disparate Society *85*

晩婚化・非婚化問題 *88*
ばんこんか ひこんかもんだい
No husbands, no wives *89*

被害者になる子供たち *92*
ひがいしゃ こども
Victimizing children *93*

暴力団撲滅 *96*
ぼうりょくだんぼくめつ
Stamping out organized crime groups *97*

オレオレ詐欺 *102*
さぎ
"It's me, it's me" frauds *103*

北朝鮮拉致問題 *106*
きたちょうせんらちもんだい
North Korean abductions *107*

捕鯨をめぐる戦い *110*
ほげい たたか
The battle over whaling *111*

生活 *Daily Life* *115*
せいかつ

コンビニエンスストア *116*
Convenience stores *117*

自動販売機 *120*
じどうはんばいき
Vending machines *121*

原発 Nuclear Power 125

原子力 126
Nuclear power 127

日本の核廃棄物の行方 130
Where does Japan's nuclear waste go? 131

東京電力 132
Tokyo Electric Power Company 133

文化 Culture 137

「おもてなし」——日本的ホスピタリティ 138
"Omotenashi": Japanese hospitality 139

和食 142
Washoku 143

旨味 146
Umami 147

職人 150
Shokunin, Japan's artisans and craftspeople 151

富士山と世界遺産 154
Mt. Fuji and World Heritage status 155

スタートは桜の花とともに 158
Starting with the cherry blossoms 159

関西VS関東 162
Kansai vs. Kanto 163

【こっか】国家

The Nation

〉〉〉 憲法改正

国家
The Nation

日本国憲法は、1947年の制定以来、アメリカの占領により「押しつけられた」ものであるという批判がなされてきた。日本人の中には、現行憲法を断固として支持する人もいれば、今こそ「より日本にふさわしい」ものにすべきだと主張する人もいる。

1990年代より、日本では戦後憲法の改正案が議論されてきている。1994年、読売新聞が憲法改正試案を掲載した。これが論憲のタブーを覆した。以来、政党各党、新聞各社、経済団体や市民社会団体などが改憲の是非を議論してきた。

□日本国憲法 Japanese Constitution
□断固として firmly
□ふさわしい suitable
□憲法改正試案 a draft for a new constitution

□論憲 discussing constitutional revision
□是非 pros and cons

>>> Revision of the Constitution

Since the Japanese Constitution was established in 1947, it has been criticized for being "imposed" by the American Occupation. Some Japanese firmly support keeping the Constitution as it is; others claim that it is time to make it "more suitable for Japan."

Beginning in the 1990s, Japan has debated proposals to revise its postwar constitution. The *Yomiuri Newspaper* published a draft for a new constitution in 1994. This broke the taboos on discussing constitutional revision. Since then, political parties, newspapers, economic organizations and civil society groups have discussed whether revisions are appropriate.

1945年9月27日、昭和天皇とGHQ総司令官ダグラス・マッカーサーとの会見
General MacArthur and the Emperor at Allied GHQ in Tokyo. September 17, 1945

もっとも多くの議論が交わされてきたのは、**戦争放棄条項**である第9条を修正すべきがどうかという問題である。同条は、日本が軍隊およびその他の戦力を持つことができないと宣言している。これを改正したい側は、国家には「**国防軍**」の設置が認められるべきだと主張している。現在、**自衛隊**には、他国から武力攻撃が加えられた場合の**国土防衛**と、国際平和維持活動（PKO）への参加が認められている。改正案は自衛隊に、国内の公の**秩序**を維持し、また個人の権利を保護する活動を認めるようである。さらには自衛隊の活動範囲も広げるようである。米国は日本に対し、**防御的役割**の拡大を望んでいる。アジア諸国は、日本の**軍備拡張**を懸念している。

改正諸案の2つ目のグループは、国民の**義務**についての議論である。現在、国民は、勤労の義務、納税の義務、その保護する子女に普通教育を受けさせる義務を負うとしている。新案は、これに国歌・国旗の**尊重**を加えている。

□戦争放棄条項 clause that renounces war
□国防軍 National Defense Force
□自衛隊 Self-Defense Force (SDF)
□国土防衛 defend Japanese territory from foreign attack

□秩序 order
□防御的役割 defense role
□軍備拡張 expansion of military
□義務 obligation
□尊重 respect

The most highly discussed issue is whether to amend Article 9, the clause that renounces war. This article declares that Japan cannot have armed forces and other war potential. Those who want to revise this say that the nation should be allowed to set up a "National Defense Force." Currently, the Self-Defense Force (SDF) is allowed to defend Japanese territory from foreign attack and participate in international peacekeeping operations (PKO). Proposed revisions would allow it to maintain domestic public order or to protect individual rights. They would also extend the scope of activities of the SDF. The U.S. would like Japan to broaden its defense role. Asian nations are worried about any expansion of Japanese military.

A second group of revisions that is discussed regards the obligations of the citizens. Currently people are required to work, to pay taxes and to ensure that children under their care receive ordinary education. New proposals include respecting the national anthem and flag.

３つ目の改正案は、**社会的儀礼**または**習俗的行為**の一部として国が**宗教的活動**を行うことを認めるものである。これはとりわけ、靖国神社参拝を公的な**追悼行為**として容認されうる慣行としたい**思惑**がある。この線に沿った改正諸案は、他のアジア諸国から否定的反応を引き出すおそれがある。

その他の改正案は、日米同盟、女性の地位、**皇位継承**、教育制度および**公益法人**を変えようとするものであった。

□ 社会的儀礼　social protocol
□ 習俗的行為　cultural practice
□ 宗教的活動　religious act
□ 追悼行為　act of remembrance
□ 思惑　aim

□ 皇位継承　imperial succession
□ 公益法人　public corporation

A third proposed revision is to allow the government to perform religious acts as part of social protocol or cultural practices. This is particularly aimed at making visits to Yasukuni Shrine an acceptable practice as a civil act of remembrance. Revisions along this line would draw negative responses from other Asian countries.

Other proposed changes would alter the U.S.-Japan Alliance, the status of women, imperial succession, the educational system, and public corporations.

国家（こっか）

The Nation

>>> 靖国神社問題

靖国神社は30年にわたり、国内外で軋轢の種となってきた。第一に、境内に併設されている資料館「遊就館」の展示が、第二次世界大戦における日本の行動を自衛によるものであったと正当化しているような印象を与えている。第二に、靖国神社は東京裁判で有罪判決を受けた14名のA級戦犯を祀っている。

靖国神社は、日本の戦死者の慰霊的な存在として、元来、そこまで物議を醸すようなことはなかった。しかし、新任の宮司が、戦争犯罪者を合祀し、1979年、そのことが一般に知れわたると、状況は変わった。日本の首相がこの神社を参拝するたびに、内外のメディアが取り上げた。歴代首相は、しばらくは誰も、私人としての参拝か、公人としての参拝かを明確にしていない。1985年、中曽根首相は初めて、首相としての参拝であることを明言した。

□軋轢の種 source of friction
□正当化する justify
□A級戦犯 Class-A war criminal
□慰霊的な memorial
□物議を醸すような controversial

□宮司 head priest
□合祀する enshrine
□参拝する go to the shrine to pay respects

>>> Yasukuni Shrine issue

Yasukuni Jinja (Yasukuni Shrine) has been a source of friction in Japan and abroad for three decades. First, the Yushukan Museum on the shrine's grounds seems to justify Japan's actions in World War II as a form of self-defense. Second, the shrine enshrines fourteen Class-A war criminals convicted at the Tokyo war crimes trials.

As a memorial for Japan's war dead, Yasukuni Shrine was originally not so controversial. But when a new head priest succeeded in having the war criminals enshrined and that became public knowledge in 1979, the situation changed. Every time a Japanese prime minister went to the shrine to pay respects, it was taken up by the media at home and abroad. For a while, prime ministers did not specify whether they were worshipping as private citizens or in their official capacity. In 1985 Prime Minister Nakasone was the first to state that he visited the shrine as prime minister.

国家 The Nation

中国、韓国などのアジア諸国は、こうした公式参拝を「軍国主義への回帰」あるいは「誤った歴史解釈」であると批判している。小泉首相は、亡くなった方々の魂に敬意の念を示し、未来の平和を祈るための手段であると、自身の参拝の弁解を試みた。ナショナリストとみなされている安倍晋三は、2012年に二度目の首相となり、引き続き「靖国問題」と向き合うことになった。2013年、終戦記念日である8月15日に首相の参拝が行われるかどうかが、特にメディアの焦点となった。自身は足を運ばなかったものの、首相は補佐を通じ、「国のために戦い、尊い命を犠牲にされた方々に対する感謝の気持ちと尊崇の念の思いを込めて」玉串料を奉納した。その年の秋季例大祭においても同じことをした。

安倍晋三首相は2013年12月26日、靖国神社を参拝した
Japan's Prime Minister Shinzo Abe visits Yasukuni Shrine on December 26, 2013

- □ 軍国主義 militarism
- □ 歴史解釈 interpretation of history
- □ 弁解する defend
- □ 終戦記念日 anniversary of the end of the war
- □ 焦点 spot particularly focused on
- □ 尊崇の念 respect
- □ 玉串料 offering

China, South Korea and other Asian nations criticize these official visits as "a return to militarism" or "an incorrect interpretation of history." Prime Minister Koizumi tried to defend his visit as a way to honor the spirits of those that died and to pray for peace in the future. When Shinzo Abe, considered a nationalist, became prime minister a second time in 2012, he continued to face the "Yasukuni problem." In 2013 the media was particularly focused on whether he would visit the shrine on August 15, the anniversary of the end of the war. He himself did not go, but he sent an aide to make an offering on his behalf "with a feeling of gratitude and respect for those who fought and gave their precious lives for their country." He did the same during the shrine's autumn festival that year.

靖国神社青銅大鳥居
The bronze torii gate at Yasukuni Shrine

››› 米軍基地

　1952年発効の日米安全保障条約は、日本の主要四島に米軍基地を置くことを認めている。基地や軍の大部分は沖縄に置かれている。

　これらの基地をめぐっては、いくつかの問題がある。1つは、自治権の問題である。国内に大規模な外国軍が駐留している日本に自治があると言えるのだろうか。これらの基地は、武力衝突が起きたとき、本当に日本を守ってくれるのだろうか。

　2つ目は、沖縄が、もっとも重い基地負担を強いられていることである。基地周辺の住民は、騒音や大気汚染、墜落事故の危険に不満の声を上げている。昼夜を問わない慢性的な航空機の騒音は、基地周辺や飛行経路の下に暮らす住民のストレスになっている。発着時に住宅地域や学校の上空を低空飛行する航空機のせいで、日常会話もままならない。これは、那覇市の北東に位置する普天間航空基地周辺で特に問題となっている。

□日米安全保障条約　The Japan-U.S. Security Treaty
□主要四島　main four islands
□自治権　autonomy
□駐留　presence

□武力衝突　military conflict
□大気汚染　air pollution
□墜落事故　aircraft crash
□慢性的な　chronic

>>> American bases

The Japan-U.S. Security Treaty of 1952 permits American bases on Japan's main four islands. A major portion of the bases and troops are in Okinawa.

There are several problems involving these bases. First, there is the issue of autonomy. How can Japan be autonomous with a large foreign military presence in the country? And will the bases actually protect Japan in case of a military conflict?

Second, Okinawa bears the harshest burden with the bases. People around the bases complain of noise, air pollution, and danger caused by aircraft. The chronic noise caused by aircraft day and night is stressful to those who live near the bases or in the flight paths. Arriving and departing aircraft fly low above residential areas and schools disrupting ordinary conversation. This is particularly problematic around Futenma Airbase, northeast of Naha.

アメリカ海軍の強襲揚陸艦キアサージ
から発艦したV-22オスプレイ
V-22 Ospreys take off from flight deck of USS keasarge

住宅地域に基地があることの危険性を知らしめたのは、2004年、普天間基地のヘリコプターが沖縄国際大学の敷地に墜落した事件である。ヘリコプターは構内の事務棟に接触した。事故歴のある垂直離着陸機オスプレイの沖縄配備が発表され、**抗議**は再燃した。2013年夏、米軍基地のヘリコプターが、市街地に近い山林に墜落し、抗議の声はさらに高まった。

3つ目は、5万人に上る沖縄駐留米軍の一部の隊員の行動に関わる問題である。日本中が**憤り**に包まれた1995年の事件では、3人の米兵が女子小学生をレイプした後、基地に逃げ帰ってしまった。それで、事件は米国の**裁判管轄**に委ねられた。レイプ、飲酒運転、住居侵入など再三にわたる米兵事件は、せめて数ヵ所だけでも沖縄から基地を移転すべきだという沖縄県民の主張をさらに**強硬**なものにしている。

北朝鮮の脅威や東シナ海の島々をめぐる領土問題の影響もあって、基地は多くの日本人にとって受け容れやすいものになってきたのかもしれない。しかし、基地の一部が国内の別の場所に移転されるか、あるいは完全に**国外移転**されない限り、沖縄県民の負担が、軽減されることはない。

□垂直着陸機　fleet of vertical lift-off　　　□国外移転する　move out of the country
□抗議　protest
□憤り　outrage
□裁判管轄　jurisdiction
□強硬な　adamant

The danger of having bases in residential areas was shown in 2004 when a U.S. helicopter from Futenma crashed on the grounds of Okinawa International University. The helicopter clipped an adminstrative office on the campus. When it was announced that a fleet of vertical lift-off Osprey aircraft, which had a record of incidents, would be stationed in Futenma, protests reignited. Protests grew even stronger in the summer of 2013 when a helicopter from the base crashed in a wooded area within sight of the city.

The third issue involves the conduct of certain members of the 50,000 troops in Okinawa. Japan was outraged in 1995 when three U.S. soldiers raped an elementary-school girl, then escaped back to their base. This put them under American jurisdiction. Repeated incidents involving U.S. troops, including rape, drunk driving, and breaking and entering, make the Okinawans more adamant that at least some bases should be moved off Okinawa.

The bases may have become more acceptable to most Japanese due to the threats of North Korea and the territorial disputes over islands in the East China Sea. But the burden on the Okinawans will not be lightened until some of those bases are moved to other parts of Japan or out of Japan completely.

>>> 皇位継承

日本の皇室はおよそ 125 代続いている。王朝としては世界最長である。過去に 8 人の女性天皇が存在したが、現行の皇室典範は、皇位を継承できるのは男系男子のみとしている。皇太子徳仁親王が雅子妃と結婚されたとき、国民は皇太子夫妻に将来日本の天皇となる男の子がすぐにできることを願った。

皇太子夫妻には、なかなか子供ができなかった。2001 年にようやく子を授かったが、生まれたのは女の赤ちゃん、愛子内親王だった。皇太子夫妻に男子の皇位継承者ができない可能性もあることがわかると、女性子孫の皇位継承を認めるために皇室典範を改正するか否かについて、国民的議論が展開された。2005 年、時の首相は女性の皇位継承を認める改正案を支持する意向を表明した。時代が変わったので「男子限定」法は改正されるべきだと考える人々からは大いなる支持を得た。一方保守派は、日本の天皇は男性の天皇であるべきだと一貫して主張していた。

□ 皇室 imperial family
□ 皇室典範 Imperial Household Law
□ 継承する take the throne
□ 皇太子 Crown Prince
□ 意向を表明する announce

□ 保守派 Conservatives
□ 一貫して continue to

>>> Imperial succession

Japan's imperial family has lasted some 125 generations. It is the longest dynasty in the world. Although there have been eight Empresses, currently the Imperial Household Law says that only males can take the throne. When Crown Prince Naruhito married Princess Masako, Japanese hoped that they would soon have a male child who could become the future Emperor of Japan.

The couple experienced difficulty in having a child. When they finally did have a child in 2001, it was a baby girl, Princess Aiko. When it became apparent that the couple might not produce a male heir, a public debate developed over whether the Imperial Household Law should be changed to allow female descendents to take the throne. In 2005 Japan's prime minister announced that he would support a bill to allow females to inherit the throne. This won significant support from those who believed that times have changed and that the "male child only" law should be revised. Conservatives, on the other hand, continued to insist that Japan should have an Emperor.

だが2006年、皇太子の弟である秋篠宮親王とその妻、紀子妃の間に男の子が生まれ、悠仁親王と名付けられた。この男の子の皇位継承順位は、伯父にあたる今上皇太子徳仁親王、そして父親の秋篠宮親王に継いで三番目となった。皇位継承に関する法律を早急に改正する必要はなくなったようである。制度改正をめぐるさまざまな議論は職場であろうと社会であろうと、あるいは皇室であろうと、女性の前に今なお立ちはだかる障壁を浮き彫りにしたようだ。日本人の大多数が、ジェンダー（性）の平等を真に理解し、推進していくには、まだ長い時間がかかるであろう。

□皇位継承順位 line of succession
□制度改正 changing the system
□障壁 barrier
□推進する promote

In 2006, however, the Crown Prince's younger brother Prince Akishino and his wife Princess Kiko gave birth to a son, named Prince Hisahito. The boy became the third in line of succession, following his uncle, the current Crown Prince Naruhito, and his father, Prince Akishino. It no longer seemed urgent to change the imperial succession law. The various arguments for and against changing the system seemed to highlight the barriers women still faced, whether at the workplace, in society or in the Imperial Household. It will be a long time before the majority of Japanese would truly understand and promote gender equality.

秋篠宮家の家紋
Japanese crest of Akishino no miya

>>> 食料自給率

国家 こっか

The Nation

　国の食料自給率とは、国内で消費されるすべての食料のうち、国内で生産された食料の割合のことである。1965年の、日本の食料自給率は73％だった。以来、食料自給率は、米消費量の減少傾向とともに下降してきた。日本人が単に以前ほど米を食べていないのである。食料自給率は、1990年代半ばからほぼ40％の横ばいで、2010年代初頭に39％に下がった。

　国は2020年までに食糧自給率を50％まで増やすことを目指している。しかしそれは、国が増産対策を講じなければ難しいだろう。1つ目の提案は、農家の収入を増やし、農家が都会の仕事に転職することなくその土地に留まるよう働きかける。2つ目は、耕作されていない土地を再生させる。農家は今も米の減反に対し補助金を受給している。使われていない土地を再び働かせることは重要である。3つ目は小規模農地を減らすこと、つまり目指すところは農地集約であり、ひいては効率の改善につながる。

□ 食料自給率 food self-sufficiency rate

□ 減少傾向 trend of declining

□ 横ばい remain at around ~

□ 増産対策 measure to increase production

□ 転職する leave for another job

□ 耕作 cultivation

□ 減反 reducing acreage

□ 補助金 subsidy

□ 農地集約 consolidate farmlands

>>> Food self-sufficiency rate

A nation's food self-sufficiency rate is the proportion of domestically produced food out of all the food that is consumed in that country. In 1965 Japan's food self-sufficiency rate stood at 73%. Since then, the rate has fallen, together with a trend of declining rice consumption. Japanese are simply not eating as much rice as they used to. From the mid-1990s on, the self-sufficiency rate has remained at around 40%, dipping to 39% in the early 2010s.

The government is aiming to raise the rate to 50% by 2020. But that will be difficult, unless the government takes measures to increase production. One proposal is to boost farmers' incomes, to encourage farmers to stay on the land, rather then leave for urban jobs. A second is to revive land that is no longer under cultivation. Until now farmers have received subsidies for reducing acreage in rice production. Putting that unused land into production again is important. A third is to reduce the amount of small-scale farm plots; the goal is to consolidate farmlands, thereby improving efficiency. A fourth is to develop new varieties of crops that are suitable for

4つ目は、加工に適した新しい作物の品種を開発する。新しい農業産品やブランド農産物は利益拡大と企業家のやる気に結びつく。

　農業は国内だけの問題ではない。食料自給率は、国の安全保障をも左右する。日本は、他国に大きく依存して生きていかなければならなくなってしまう。今のところは、海外各国から必要な食料・食品を買い入れることができている。だが今後とも、日本がこれまでと同じようにやっていけるかどうかはわからない。

□作物　agricultural product
□利益拡大　increase profit
□左右する　affect
□依存する　dependent on

processing. New agricultural products and brand-name products increases profits and encourages entrepreneurs.

Agriculture is not merely a domestic issue. Food self-sufficiency affects national security. It makes Japan more dependent on other nations for its own survival. So far, Japan has been able to purchase necessary foods and food products from various countries. Whether Japan can continue to do so remains to be seen.

›››かっこいい日本

　かつては**経済大国**として知られた日本だが、ここ 10 年はクールな (カッコいい) ものといえば日本として知られるようになってきた。この**概念**は、ジャーナリスト、ダグラス・マクグレイが 2002 年に発表した「日本のグロス・ナショナル・クール」と題する記事から進化したものである。マクグレイは、日本がいかにして、その**経済的優位性を喪失**しつつも「クール」なソフトパワーの**国際的な発信源**へと**変容**していったかを書いている。記事は、アニメ、漫画、J-POP、家電製品、ストリートファッション、ハローキティ (正式名称キティ・ホワイト) の可愛さについても触れている。

□経済大国 economic superpower
□概念 concept
□経済的優位性 economic dominance
□喪失する lose
□発信源 source

□変容する transform

❯❯❯ "Cool Japan"

Although Japan was once known as an economic superpower, in the past decade it has become known as the epitome of what is cool. The concept evolved from an article published in 2002 by journalist Douglas McGray titled "Japan's Gross National Cool." McGray was writing about how Japan had lost its economic edge but had transformed into an international source of "cool" soft power. His article mentioned anime, manga, J-pop, consumer electronics, street fashion, and the cuteness of Hello Kitty, whose full name is Kitty White.

Japan Expo「Village Japon」(2011年フランス)にて、日本のアニメソングを演奏する奈良県のステージ

Photograph taken during the 12th edition of Japan Expo in 2011 organised at the 'Parc de expositions of Villepinte near Paris in France.
Yves Tennevin

意外にも素早く、日本の政府は文化輸出と日本への観光を促進するためのスローガンとして「クールジャパン」を推奨し始めた。日本の公共放送 NHK は、『COOLJAPAN 発掘！ かっこいいニッポン』というタイトルの長期番組を展開した。この番組には世界各国の外国人が登場して、古いものから新しいものまで日本の風習についてコメントするのだが、結論は必ずそれが「クール」だということにたどりつく。

特に 3.11（東日本大震災）以後の日本経済を立て直すための動きとして、国や企業はもっと「クールジャパン」を支援すべきだという人々もいる。また「クールジャパン」ブームはもう終わったと指摘する人々もいる。だがよくよく観察すれば、日本には、**創造性**にあふれた**職人**、アーティスト、デザイナー、映画監督、漫画家がいて、日本の**枠を越えた**強烈な魅力を放っていることがわかる。そうした人々が海外のファンを獲得できるようサポートすることは、今後とも日本の経済に良い効果をもたらすだけでなく、日本のイメージアップにもつながるかもしれない。

□ 促進する promote
□ 発掘する discover
□ 長期番組 long-running series
□ 創造性 creativity
□ 職人 craftspeople

□ 枠を越えた beyond the border

Rather quickly, the national government began pushing "Cool Japan" as a slogan to promote cultural exports and incoming tourism. The national public broadcaster NHK developed a long-running series called "Cool Japan Hakkutsu." The program featured foreigners from a variety of countries commenting on customs, long-standing and new, and inevitably coming to the conclusion that Japan was "cool."

Some say that the government and corporations should offer more support to "Cool Japan" as a movement to rebuild Japan's economy, especially after 3.11 (The Great East Japan Earthquale in 2011). Others point out that the "Cool Japan" boom is over. But the wisest observers say that Japan has creative craftspeople, artists, designers, movie directors, and cartoonists who have great appeal beyond Japan's borders. Helping those people reach audiences abroad could continue to help Japan's image as well as its economy.

››› 日本の「幸福度ランキング」

　日本は、経済協力開発機構 (OECD) 加盟国である 34 か国の一つである。OECD は、「より良い暮らし指標」(国民の幸福度の比較指標値) として知られる調査を公表している。2011 年の調査を見ると、日本にとっては喜ばしいことが多い。とりわけ世帯所得、卒業率、平均寿命が OECD の平均より高い。

　しかし日本人は「幸せ」なのだろうか。OECD 加盟国全体で、今の生活に満足していると答えた人の平均は 59％だった。高い健康水準や教育水準、相対的に良い給料にもかかわらず、満足していると答えた日本人はわずか 40％に過ぎない。これと比較して、オランダでは 91％、カナダでは 78％、オーストラリアでは 75％の国民が満足していると答えている。日本人は、自分たちが手にしているものに満足していないようである。

□指標 index
□世帯所得 household income
□卒業率 graduation rate
□平均寿命 life expectancy
□水準 level

□相対的に relatively

>>> Japan's "Happiness Rank"

Japan is one of 34 member countries belonging to the Organization for Economic Co-operation and Development (OECD). The OECD publishes a survey known as the Better Life Index, a comparative index of national happiness. According to the 2011 survey, Japan has a lot to be grateful for. It is higher than the OECD average in household income, graduation rates and life expectancy, among others.

But are the Japanese "happy"? The average of people in all OECD countries who said that they were satisfied with their current life was 59%. Despite good health, high education, and relatively high salaries, only 40% of Japanese said that they were satisfied. In comparison, 91% of Dutch citizens, 78% of Canadians and 75% of Australians said they were satisfied. It seems that the Japanese aren't happy with what they have.

国家 こうか

The Nation

【せいじ】政治

Politics

政治
せいじ
Politics

>>> 領土問題

東シナ海には、日本語で尖閣諸島、中国語で钓鱼岛（日本名：魚釣島）と呼ばれる島嶼群があり、両国間で軋轢の種になってきた。これらの島々は、日本が**実効支配**しているが、中国はこれらの島々を中国の領土であると主張しており、台湾も同様に**領有権**を主張している。2010年、中国の漁船が海上保安庁の**巡視船**に追跡され、同諸島付近で巡視船に衝突した。日本の巡視船は、漁船とその船長・船員を**拿捕**した。この行動に対し中国各都市で、大規模な抗議行動が起こり、現地日系企業が被害を受けた。最終的に、船員は**釈放**され、船も返還された。

□ 実効支配 control
□ 領有権 dominium
□ 巡視船 patrol vessel
□ 拿捕する seize
□ 釈放する release

46

>>> Disputed territories

In the East China Sea, a group of islands, called the Senkaku Islands in Japanese and the Diaoyu Islands in Chinese, has become a source of friction between the two countries. Japan controls the islands, but China claims they are Chinese territory, and Republic of China claims them, too. In 2010 a Chinese fishery vessel being pursued by a Japanese Coast Guard vessel rammed the Japanese ship near the islands. The Japanese vessel seized the boat, its captain and its crew. Massive protests broke out in Chinese cities against this action, with damage done to Japanese-owned businesses. Eventually the crew and ship were released.

尖閣諸島魚釣島
©国土交通 省
Uotsuri shima

これらの島々は基本的に人が住むには適さないが、支配する国に排他的な経済的利権を約束するため、きわめて高い価値を持っている。8つの島・岩礁の下には、膨大な石油とガスが埋蔵されているのである。2012年に東京都知事が、個人所有の3つの島を都に購入させる意向を表明し、再び緊張が高まった。その翌年には、日本の文部科学省が、問題の島々を日本の領土と主張している地理および政治経済の教科書を検定合格としたことに対し、中国政府が抗議を行った。

もう1つの領土問題は、日本海にある岩礁の群島、竹島に関するもので、韓国が実効支配し、韓国語では独島として知られている。この領土問題は、歴史の記憶と解釈の問題である。竹島／独島は、1954年に韓国に不法占拠された。それ以来、両国の漁業関係者らは、島の周辺海域を共有することで合意しようとしてきた。しかし、どちらの国が実際に島々を所有しているかという議論においては、ほとんど進展がみられなかった。

これらの領土問題の後ろには、いわゆる「北方領土問題」が控えている。北海道の東端にある島々に絡む問題で、ロシアが占領し、日本が領有権を主張している。

□ 排他的な exclusive

□ 埋蔵する bury

□ 検定合格とする approve

□ 記憶と解釈 memory and interpretation

□ 不法占拠する seize illegally

□ 合意する reach an agreement

Although fundamentally uninhabitable, these islands are extremely valuable for the exclusive economic rights they guarantee to the nation that controls them. The eight islands and rocky islets sit atop vast oil and gas reserves. When the governor of Tokyo stated his intention to have Tokyo buy three of the privately owned islands in 2012, tensions reheated. The following year the Chinese government protested when the Japanese education ministry approved textbooks in geography and politics and economics claiming the disputed islands as Japanese territories.

A second dispute involves Takeshima in the Sea of Japan, a chain of islets controlled by South Korea and known in Korean as the Dokdo Islands. This dispute is a matter of historical memory and interpretation. Takeshima/Dokdo was seized by South Korea in 1954. Since then, fishing communities in the two countries have tried to reach an agreement to share the waters around the islands. But little progress was made in discussing who actually owned the islands.

In the background of these disputes is the so-called "Northern Territories issue." This involves islands off the east coast of Hokkaido, which Russia occupies and which Japan claims.

政治せいじ

Politics

›››謝罪と戦争責任

アジアの中のある国々は、日本が第二次世界大戦中のアジアにおける行為に対し責任を取っていないと度々主張している。領土問題が起きる、あるいは日本国憲法改正が話題となるとき、その陰には、常にこの主張がある。

実は、日本は、戦争を起こし近隣諸国を苦しめたことに対し謝罪をしてきている。日本の歴代首相は、自国の犯した過ちについて謝罪の意を表明してきた。世論調査は、多くの日本人が、日本はアジアにおいて謝罪するに値する行為をしたと感じていることを示している。

日本の「誠意」に対する不信感は、複数の要因によるものである。第一に、ある政治家たちが、日本の歴史の教科書を「より否定的色合いの薄い」ものにしようと提唱していることがある。第二に、日本が被害者、特に第二次世界大戦中の日本軍のためのいわゆる「慰安婦」に対する補償について、これといった対応をしてきていないことがある。

□度々 frequently
□謝罪の意 apology
□世論調査 opinion poll
□誠意 sincerity
□不信感 doubt

□被害者 victim
□慰安婦 comfort women
□補償 compensation

>>> Apologies and war responsibility

Certain Asian nations frequently claim that Japan has not taken responsibility for what it did in Asia during World War II. When disputes arise over territory or the topic of changing the Japanese constitution comes up, this claim is consistently in the background.

Actually, Japan has apologized for waging war and oppressing its neighbors. Japanese prime ministers have offered apologies for their country's misdeeds. Opinion polls show that most Japanese feel that Japan did things in Asia that it should apologize for.

Doubts about Japanese "sincerity" result from multiple factors. First, some politicians call for making Japanese history textbooks "less negative." Second, Japan has not done much in the way of offering compensation to the victims, especially the so-called "comfort women" for Japanese troops during World War II.

第三に、日本の**古参**の政治家たちがしばしば、日本人の心からの**謝罪の意を弱める**ような発言を口にすることである。たとえば、森喜朗元首相は、日本が天皇を中心としている**神の国**であると、まるで戦時中のナショナリズムのような発言をした。2013 年には麻生太郎外相が、誰も気づかないうちにドイツの憲法を変えたナチスの**手口**に学んだらどうかと述べた。彼の歴史に対する理解不足を示したようなものだ。こうした発言が、戦時中の行き過ぎた行為に対する日本の謝罪に「誠意が感じられない」と考える周辺アジア諸国を正当化している。

だが、受け入れられないなら謝罪をする意味はない。おそらく、いかなる謝罪も**抗議する**国々を満足させることはできないのだろう。それゆえ日本の政治家は、諸外国との**関係進展**につながらない謝罪表明や補償の申し出をしてまで、国内のナショナリストたちを刺激しようとは思わないのである。

□古参の senior

□意を弱める undercut a sense

□神の国 country of the gods

□手口 deception

□抗議する protest

□関係進展 advance relations

Third, senior Japanese politicians often make comments that undercut the sense that Japanese are really sorry. Prime Minister Yoshiro Mori, for example, commented that Japan was a country of the gods with the Emperor at its center, which sounded like wartime nationalism. In 2013 Foreign Minister Taro Aso suggested that Japan might take a hint from the Nazis who managed to change Germany's constitution without being noticed. This suggested that he lacked an understanding of history. Japan's Asian neighbors are justified in seeing these comments as showing "a lack of sincerity" in Japan's apologies for its wartime excesses.

In contrast, there is no point in apologizing if it will not be accepted. Perhaps no apology would be enough to satisfy the protesting nations. Therefore, Japanese politicians are not willing to irritate Japanese nationalists to make an apology and offer compensation that will not advance relations with other countries.

ビルマ（現ミャンマー）の連合国軍キャンプで尋問を待つ慰安婦とされる女性

A young woman who was in one of the "comfort women" is interviewed by an Allied officer in Bulma

【けいざい】 経済

Economics

>>> 年金危機

　日本はかつて事実上の「終身雇用」で知られ、年金は退職者の基本的ニーズを充分満たしていた。実際のところ「終身雇用」は決して普遍的な制度ではなかった。大企業にはその慣行があったが、中小企業には、そのような保証はなかった。大企業はまた、退職した社員に年金を約束していたが、その年金の財源がいま問題化している。

　最終的な社会保障のセーフティネットは、日本国民年金制度である。しかし同制度には問題が生じている。まず、2007年の大きな不祥事では、社会保険庁の記録が不完全で、年金納入者の正確な記録がないことが発覚した。加えて急速な高齢化という問題があり、縮小する若年層の働き手が増え続ける高齢退職者層のために年金制度を支えていかなければならない。

□ 終身雇用 lifetime employment
□ 年金 pension
□ 退職者 retiree
□ 普遍的な universal

□ 日本国民年金制度 Japan's national pension system
□ 不祥事 scandal
□ 高齢退職者層 elderly retirees

›› National pension crisis

Japan was once known for virtual "lifetime employment" and a pension sufficient to meet the basic needs of retirees. Actually, "lifetime employment" was never a universal system. Large companies maintained the practice, but medium and small companies did not make that guarantee. Large companies also promised pensions to their retired employees, but funding those pensions has become problematic.

The ultimate social security safety net has been Japan's national pension system, *kokumin nenkin seido*. But that system is in trouble. First, in a major scandal in 2007, it became known that the Social Insurance Agency did not have complete, accurate records of who had paid into the system. Second, the rapid aging of society means that a smaller percentage of young workers would have to contribute to a fund for an ever-increasing percentage of elderly retirees.

この負担を軽減するための対策として、**満額支給**の開始年齢が60歳から65歳に引き上げられた。さらに国は、65歳に達する者に対し**繰り下げた**月数分増額受給できるとし、受給開始時期の繰り下げを**奨励**している。

年金問題は出生率の低下や、女性の雇用および出産後の**職場復帰**を認める法律や企業方針の修正とも密接な関係がある。さらにそれは、**保育・託児施設**の整備にも結びついている。それゆえ、年金問題はより大きな社会問題の**一端に過ぎない**のである。

経済 けいざい
Economics

□満額支給 full payment
□繰り下げる delay
□奨励する encourage
□職場復帰 return to work
□保育・託児施設 child care center

□一端に過ぎない be only part of ~

In an effort to reduce this burden, the age of eligibility for full pension payments has been raised from 60 to 65. Further, the government is encouraging those who turn 65 to wait to receive payments by promising higher amounts for each month they delay.

This issue is closely tied to the decreased birthrate and changing laws and company policies to allow women to join and stay in the workforce after giving birth. That, in turn, is tied with making child care centers more available. The pension system, therefore, is only part of larger social issues.

日本年金機構本部
Japan Pension Service building in Tokyo

経済
けいざい
Economics

>>> 働く女性
はたら　じょせい

　従来の女性観である「良妻賢母」は時代遅れとなった。夫婦共じゅうらい　じょせいかん　　　　　りょうさいけんぼ　　　　　　じだいおく　　　　　　ふうふとも働き世帯など今どきふつうである。女性は、世帯収入にかなりばたら　せたい　　いま　　　　　　　　　　じょせい　　せたいしゅうにゅうの貢献をしている。職場においても女性の受け入れは進んでいこうけん　　　　　　　　しょくば　　　　　　じょせい　　う　い　　すする。

　それでもなお、目に見えない障壁が職場における男女平等を　　　　　　　　　め　み　　　　しょうへき　しょくば　　　　　　だんじょびょうどう阻害している。日本は諸外国に遅れをとっている。日本の女性のそがい　　　　　　にほん　しょがいこく　おく　　　　　　　　　　にほん　じょせい労働人口はおよそ48%、米国では約58%である。しかし、日本のろうどうじんこう　　　　　　べいこく　やく　　　　　　　　　　　にほん大卒女性の70%以上は子供を持つと仕事をやめる。対する米国だいそつじょせい　　　いじょう　こども　も　　しごと　　　　たい　　べいこくでは、その割合は約30%である。わりあい　やく

　日本の女性が職場を離れるのは、子育てや年老いた親の世話をにほん　じょせい　しょくば　はな　　　　　こそだ　　としお　　おや　せわするためである。こうした負担のせいで、多くの女性が退職を余ふたん　　　　　おお　じょせい　たいしょく　よ儀なくされ、その後も復職できない。ある調査によると働く女性ぎ　　　　　ご　ふくしょく　　　　　ちょうさ　　　はたら　じょせいの数が増えれば、日本はGDPを15%近く伸ばすことができるとかず　ふ　　　　にほん　　　　　　　ちか　のいう。解決に向けて、いくつかの提案もなされてきている。かいけつ　む　　　　　　ていあん

□ 良妻賢母　good wife, wise mother
□ 夫婦共働き世帯　double-income household
□ 貢献をする　contribute
□ 阻害する　prevent

□ 遅れをとる　be behind
□ ～を余儀なくされる　have no choice but to

>>> Women in the workforce

The traditional view of the woman as "good wife, wise mother" is outdated. Double-income households are now quite common. Women contribute an important amount to the family income. They are gaining acceptance in the workplace as well.

Yet there is an invisible barrier that prevents gender equality at work. Japan is behind other countries. Some 48% of adult Japanese women are in the labor force, compared to about 58% in the U.S. But over 70% of women in Japan with college degrees quit when they have children. That compares to about 30% in the U.S.

Japanese women drop out of the workforce to take care of their children and to take care of their aging parents. These responsibilities cause many to leave and not return to work later. According to research, Japan could increase its GDP by almost 15% if the number of working women increased. Several solutions have been proposed.

１つ目は、働く母親のために託児サービスを提供すること。2つ目は、国家公務員の女性採用に際しクォータ制を設けること。3つ目は、フレックスタイム制を導入し、働く女性たちやその夫たちが放課後の子供の面倒を見ることができるようにすることである。

□託児サービス　day care for children
□国家公務員　government official
□導入する　create, introduce
□放課後　after school

One is to provide day care for children of working mothers. A second is to establish a quota system for hiring women in government jobs. A third is to create flexible working schedules that would allow working women and their husbands to take care of their children after school.

>>> 築地移転

経済 *Economics*

築地は、世界最大の魚市場である。海外からの観光客にとっても観光の目玉になってきた。旅行者たちは朝早起きして、高価な冷凍マグロの殺気立った競りや、日本刀のような包丁を使ったマグロの解体を見学する。だが、もうすぐそれもなくなってしまう。市場移転の決定が初めて発表されたときには、反対が起きた。築地市場は80年近くにわたり、都内に向けた鮮魚等水産物の流通の拠点となってきた。移転先予定地は精製工場跡地であり、有害な化学物質が残っていることが判明した。市場業者らは、市場で働く人たちの間で築き上げられてきた伝統や文化だけでなく、自分たちの生活まで破壊される可能性があると主張した。東京が前回の五輪招致の際に落選したときは、つかの間ではあったがほっとした空気があった。だが東京が2020年の五輪候補地に決定されるとともに築地の運命も決まってしまった。市場は、銀座などからもっと離れた埋立地の人工島に移される予定である。

□ 目玉　main attraction
□ 殺気立った　frantic
□ 解体　carving
□ 鮮魚等水産物　fresh fish and other marine products
□ 流通の拠点　logistics base
□ 精製工場跡地　land after the refinery
□ 有害な化学物質　toxic chemical
□ 伝統や文化　traditional and culture
□ 五輪招致　bid for the Olympic games
□ 埋立地　reclaimed land

>>> Moving Tsukiji

Tsukiji is the world's largest fish market. It has become a major sightseeing attraction for visitors from abroad. These travelers get up early in the morning to see the frantic auction of expensive frozen tuna and the carving of the tuna with knives that look like swords. Soon, this will disappear.

There was resistance when the decision to move the market was first announced. The Tsukiji market has been the source of fresh fish and other marine products to Tokyo for close to 80 years. The proposed site for relocation was found to have toxic chemicals remaining from the refinery that had previously occupied it. The merchants claimed that it would destroy their livelihood as well as the traditional culture that had built up among those who work there. When Tokyo lost its first bid for the Olympic games, there was a temporary sense of relief. But with the designation of Tokyo as the site of the 2020 Olympics, Tsukiji's fate has been finalized. The market will be moved to an island of reclaimed land further away from the Ginza area.

市場移転後の跡地は高層マンション群に再開発される予定であり、五輪用地となる人工島を結ぶトンネルの建設も予定されている。反対派は、官僚たちが自分たちの昔からの支援基盤である不動産開発業者や大手建設業者を儲けさせたいだけという。

予定地では汚染土壌が削りとられ、きれいな土壌と入れ替えられている。新しい市場は、近代的で温度管理のなされた物流センターとなる。

移転されない「場外」が、どうなるかは今のところ不明である。市場がなくなった後、場外の店舗や屋台のオーナーたちは、顧客を引きつけることができるだろうか。

□再開発する redevelop
□五輪用地 site of the Olympic event
□官僚 bureaucrat
□支援基盤 support base
□汚染土壌 contaminated soil

□顧客 customer

The old site is to be redeveloped into high-rise apartment buildings, and a tunnel will be built to connect the islands that will house the sites of the Olympic events. Opponents say that Japanese bureaucrats simply want to enrich real estate developers and the big construction companies, their traditional support base.

The contaminated soil of the new location is being scraped away and replaced with clean dirt. The new market will be a modern, climate-controlled distribution center.

It remains to be seen what happens to the *jogai*, outside market, that will not be moved. Will the shop and stall owners be able to attract customers once the market is gone?

築地中央卸売市場での冷凍マグロのセリ
Tuna Auctions at Tsukiji Fish Market

経済 Economics

67

≫ 老舗

「老舗」と呼ばれる商店やレストランなどの伝統的なビジネスが提供する商品やサービスには、数世代にわたり蓄積されてきた技術、製法、調理法、ノウハウが注ぎ込まれている。

老舗に共通する特徴には、数世代に及ぶ専門知識の集約が挙げられる。店の営業年数については決まった定義がないが、一般的には70年〜300年といったところだろう。また老舗は、今でも創業者の一族が所有・経営しているところがほとんどである。一族は、多くの場合人と技術に大きく依存した昔ながらの生産技術を維持している。そうした技術は、書いて覚えるようなものではない。見習いの人間が感覚や見た目、味、あるいは勘によってその製品が基準に達しているかわかるようになるまで、直接指導することで、習得されていくのである。

□老舗 long-established enterprise

□蓄積する accumulate

□定義 definition

□見習いの人間 apprentice

□勘 intuition

>>> *Shinise,* long-established enterprises

Techniques, formulas, recipes and know-how accumulated over several generations go into products and services offered by shops, restaurants and other traditional businesses referred to as *shinise.*

The specific characteristics generally include a gathering of expertise over several generations. There is no set definition for how long the shop has been in operation, but somewhere between 70 and 300 years is the general range. And almost all of these shops are still owned and operated by the family that founded the business. The family has carried on the traditional production techniques which are often labor-intensive and skill-intensive. These skills are usually not written down. They are acquired by direct instruction until the apprentice knows by feel, by eye, by taste or by intuition that the product is up to standard.

店名や商標が代々続いているあかしは、店の入口に垂れ下がっている伝統的な布（暖簾）に象徴されることが多い。「暖簾を守る」という言い回しは、良き伝統を存続させるという意味である。代々守って行くべき信条を明文化している店もあれば、口頭で伝えていく店もある。

老舗の中には、昔ながらの店を大企業へと成長させたところもあり、1673年に呉服屋として創業し、百貨店の代表格へと成長してきた三越がその良い例である。典型的な老舗はもっと小規模で、日本酒の蔵元、和菓子やお茶、漬物、調味料、佃煮を売る店などがある。

老舗という尊称に値する店は、自分たちで、そして自分たちだけで完成させた製法や技術、調理法を発展させてきた。同じ品は他では見つからない。老舗にはその店に信頼を寄せる安定した客層もある。代々同じ品を求めてやって来る顧客がいることもある。

□商標 brand
□あかし testament
□暖簾 curtain
□象徴する symbolize
□信条 creed

□明文化する write out
□呉服屋 traditional clothing shop
□尊称 complimentary title

This continuity of name and brand is often symbolized by the traditional curtain (*noren*) at the shop entrance. "Protecting the *noren*" (*noren o mamoru*) is the expression used for keeping the good traditions alive. Some shops have a written creed that each generation is to follow; others have a creed that is passed down verbally.

Some *shinise* developed from traditional shops into major businesses, such as Mitsukoshi, which began as a traditional clothing shop in 1673 and has evolved into an iconic department store. The more typical shops are smaller, including saké makers and sellers of *wagashi* (Japanese-style confections), green tea, *tsukemono* (pickled vegetables), seasonings, and *tsukudani* (food boiled in soy).

Shops that qualify for the complimentary *shinise* designation have developed a formula, technique or recipe that they—and only they—have achieved. It is not possible to find the same product anywhere else. They have a stable clientele who count on the reliability of the shop. In some cases customers come generation after generation for the same goods.

【しゃかい】社会

Society

>>> 人口高齢化

社会
Society

　「高齢化社会」とは、65歳以上の国民が総人口の7%を超える社会のことである。「高齢社会」とは、人口の14%が65歳以上の社会のことである。日本の人口は、世界のどの国よりも急速に「高齢化」している──**断**トツである。第二次世界大戦前の日本人は平均して、55歳あるいは60歳で退職した後、**せいぜい**数年生きられるかといった状況だった。現在、日本人の平均寿命は、退職してから20年近く、女性は83歳、男性は79歳である。これが進むと、2025年には、日本は世界でもっとも**逆三角形化**の進んだ人口ピラミッドを**抱える**ことになると予測されている。

□高齢化社会　aging society
□断トツ　bar none
□せいぜい　only ~ at most
□逆三角形　upside-down triangle
□抱える　have

>>> Graying of the population

Koreika shakai, an "aging society," is a society in which citizens aged 65 or older rise above 7% of the total population. An "aged society" is one in which 14% of the population is 65 or older. The Japanese population is "graying" faster than any other country in the world—bar none. In the pre-World War II period, the average Japanese could expect to live only a few years past retirement at 55 or 60. Now, the average Japanese can expect to live close to two decades past retirement age, to age 83 for women and to 79 for men. As a result, it is estimated that by 2025 Japan will have the most top-heavy population pyramid in the world.

国は、高齢者のための年金、住宅、医療および**福祉制度**に、より多くの予算を投入せねばならなくなる。2000 年に**施行**された長期の**介護保険制度**は、来るべき変化の 1 つの**先触れ**である。この介護保険制度では、退職する人もいる 65 歳から**保険料**を納めなくてはならない。2 つ目の変化として、年金受給開始年齢の段階的な引き上げがあり、最初は 60 歳から 65 歳だったが、ゆくゆくはさらに引き上げられるだろう。

　こうした高齢者の面倒は、誰が見るのだろうか。子供がいたとしても、フルタイムで仕事をしていれば、親が病気になっても介護のために家にいることはできない。普通の病院には、病気の患者用にスペースが限られている。「高齢」だけが問題の患者を**無期限**に受け入れようとはしたがらない。

□福祉制度 welfare program
□施行する go into effect
□介護保険制度 care insurance system
□先触れ sign
□保険料 insurance premium

□無期限に indefinitely

The government will have to spend more money on pensions, housing, medical care and welfare programs for the senior citizens. The long-term care insurance system which went into effect in 2000 is a sign of the changes that will come. In this system, people who reach the age of 65 have to pay insurance premiums at a time when some are leaving the work force. A second change is the gradual raising of the age of eligibility for pension payments, first from 60 to 65 and eventually higher.

Who will take care of these senior citizens? If they have children, those children have full-time jobs and cannot stay home to care for parents who become invalids. Hospitals have limited space for people with medical problems. These hospitals are unwilling to let patients stay indefinitely if their only problem is "old age."

社会
しゃかい
Society

≫≫ 人口減少
じんこうげんしょう

　国のある調査機関によると、2040年には日本の人口は現在の
1億2700万人から約1億700万人まで落ちこむという。さらに
2060年にはその人口は約8700万人になると推定されている。
　それが日本にとって何を意味するかといえば、国内のいたると
ころで平均年齢が上がるということである。2040年には、**全都道**
府県で人口の30%以上が65歳以上になるという。北海道、東北
地方の大部分、日本海側の各県、四国および九州の大部分は、
2010年と比較して、人口の20%以上を失うことになる。
　数字は**深刻**そうだが、**具体的には**何を意味しているのだろうか。

□ 調査機関 research center
□ 全都道府県 all prefectures of Japan
□ 深刻 troubling
□ 具体的には exactly, specifically

>>> Shrinking population

By 2040, according to a national research center, Japan's population will drop from the current 127 million to about 107 million. Further, by 2060, that population is estimated to be about 87 million.

What this means to the country is that the average age will be higher everywhere. In 2040, more than 30% of the population in every prefecture will be age 65 or older. Hokkaido, most of Tohoku and the prefectures along the Sea of Japan, Shikoku, and most of Kyushu will lose more than 20% of their population, compared with 2010.

These figures sound troubling, but what exactly do they mean?

１つの影響は、公的なサービス、特に医療・介護サービスの需要がますます高まることである。これにはさらに経費がかかるようになるだろうが、人口が減るにしたがって、総税収は減少する。のちのち税金を納め、公的サービスの費用を負担してくれるような労働力を増やすことが重要になる。女性や外国人労働者をできる限り早期に労働力として取り入れることが重要なのはそのためでもある。

　もう１つの影響は、インフラ需要の転換である。小学校の需要は縮小し、高齢者向け施設の需要が増加する。高齢者は、一ヵ所でさまざまなサービスを受けられるような施設の近くに転居しなくてはならなくなる。

　道路を走る車の数は減るだろうし、道路工事も少なくなるだろう。交通量や予算が少ないせいで、トンネルや橋梁が使われなくなるかもしれない。都市部の公共交通機関にしても、運賃を払って乗る乗客が減少する中で維持していかなければならなくなる。

□需要 need

□経費 cost

□総税収 total tax revenue

□外国人労働者 foreign worker

□転換 shift

□橋梁 bridge

□公共交通機関 public transportation

One impact will be an ever-increasing need for social services, especially medical and nursing care services. This will cost more money, but as the population decreases, total tax revenues will decline. It will become important to increase the workforce, which will then pay taxes, which will in turn pay for the social services. This is one reason why it is important to get women and foreign workers into the workforce as early as possible.

Another impact will be a shift in infrastructure needs. There will be decreased need for elementary schools and increased need for facilities for the elderly. The elderly will have to be relocated closer to more centralized facilities where they can be taken care of.

There will be a decrease in the number of vehicles on the roads and road maintenance will decline. Tunnels and bridges may be closed due to lack of traffic and funding. Public transportation in the urban areas will have to be maintained with fewer passengers paying to ride.

国全体の**過疎化**を**食い止める**ために、日本は何ができるだろうか。21世紀の変わり目に、**国連**の報告書が興味深い提案をした。それによると、現在の労働人口を維持するためには、日本は、2050年まで毎年60万人近い**移民**を受け入れる必要があるという。日本に、それだけの数の海外からの労働者を受け入れる**政治的意思**があるのかは疑問である。

□ 過疎化 depopulation
□ 食い止める prevent
□ 国連 United Nations
□ 移民 immigrant
□ 政治的意思 political will

What can Japan do to prevent depopulation of the entire country? At the turn of the 21st century, a report from the United Nations made an interesting suggestion. To maintain the current working population, it said, Japan would need to accept some 600,000 immigrants per year until 2050. Whether Japan has the political will to admit that many workers from abroad is doubtful.

社会 しゃかい

Society

>>> 格差社会

社会
Society

1980年代まで多くの日本人は、自分が中流階級に属していると考えていた。しかし、1990年代初頭にバブルが崩壊し、日本が最初のいわゆる「失われた10年」に突入すると、その見方は変わり始めた。長期にわたる景気低迷の結果、約束されていた終身雇用モデルの崩壊が始まった。中流階級が縮小しはじめた。

2000年代初頭、日本はトップと底辺で経済レベルの開きが大きくなる「格差社会」へと変容しはじめた。1つの原因は、教育レベルの違いだった。学習塾に通う経済的余裕がなく、一流大学に入ることができなかった人々は、安定した職を得ることができなかった。

□中流階級 middle class
□バブル economic bubble
□景気低迷 recession
□底辺 bottom
□格差社会 society with a widening gap

□安定した職 secure employment

>>> Disparate Society

Until the 1980s, most Japanese thought that they belonged to the middle class. When the bubble collapsed in the early 1990s and Japan entered the first so-called "lost decade," however, that view began to change. As a result of the long recession, the promised life-time employment model started to collapse. The middle class began to shrink.

In the early 2000s, Japan started to become a *kakusa shakai*, a society with a widening gap between the top and the bottom economic levels. One cause was a difference in education level. Those who could not afford cram schools and could not get into top universities could not get secure employment.

今日の若年労働者層は、正社員と**非正規就業者**のグループに分断されているようである。2001年から2006年の間に、正社員数は190万人落ち込み、非正規就業者の数は330万人増加した。大学卒業者でさえ、安定した企業で正社員の職を得るために**悪戦苦闘**していた。

　家庭においても変化がみられた。かつて**既婚女性**は夫が一日中働いている間、家で子育てや家事を引き受けた。その後、女性が男性と同じようにキャリアを追い求める時代が訪れた。彼女たちは当然のことながら、自分の持っている能力を生かし、リーダー的役割を担いたいと思った。しかし近年は、**家計を助ける**という別の目的で働いている。これは生活費の高さが一因にある。男性の雇用形態が変化したことも大きい。多くの夫が、収入を減らされたり、解雇されたり、非正規雇用でありながらフルタイムで働いたりしている。夫婦の多くが共働きの必要を感じている。子供をもうける**余裕がない**と感じている夫婦も多い。保育・託児施設の不足も**二の足を踏ませる**原因になっている。

□非正規就業者 temporary worker
□悪戦苦闘する struggle
□既婚女性 married woman
□家計を助ける contribute to the household income

□余裕がない cannot afford to
□二の足を踏ませる discourage

Young workers today seem to be divided into the full-time employee and temporary worker groups. Between 2001 and 2006, the population of the regular-employed fell by 1.9 million, and the population of temporary workers rose by 3.3 million. Even university graduates struggled to find full-time jobs with dependable companies.

There were also changes in the Japanese home. In the past, married women stayed at home and took care of the children and housework while their husbands worked all day. Then came a period when women sought careers just like men. They naturally wanted to use the abilities they had to take leadership roles. Recently, however, there is a new reason for working: to contribute to the household income. This is partly due to high living expenses. Significantly, it has been due to a change in employment status of the men. Many husbands are earning less, suffering layoffs or working full-time shifts as temporary workers. Many couples feel they both have to work. And many feel that they cannot afford to have children. The lack of child care centers discourages them, too.

>>> 晩婚化・非婚化問題

多くの先進諸国がそうであるように、日本でも平均初婚年齢が上がっている。厚生労働省によると、男性の平均初婚年齢は31歳、女性の平均初婚年齢は29歳である。国が憂慮するのは、出生率低下の問題があるからである。日本の人口は急速に高齢化しており、高齢の国民が退職し年金を国から引き出す一方で、税金を納め国民年金制度に拠出する若い働き手はさらに少なくなっていく。日本には、子供がもっと必要である。

日本人の間で婚期が遅れているのは、さまざまな要因が影響しているようである。結婚し子供を持つのは当然という社会の圧力は、ここ数十年で明らかに減少してきた。より多くの女性が仕事を持ちたいと考えているが、それは女性が結婚して、夫に経済的に依存する必要が少なくなっているということである。一方で、長期にわたる景気後退の結果、男性は家族を養っていく上で満足できるほど充分な収入を得ていないことが多い。

□ 晩婚化　tendency to late marriage
□ 非婚化　tendency to unmarry
□ 平均初婚年齢　average age of first marriage
□ 憂慮する　concern
□ 拠出する　pay
□ 婚期　marriageable age
□ 景気後退　economic recession

❯❯❯ No husbands, no wives

The average age of first marriage is rising in Japan, just as it is in many other advanced nations. According to the Health, Labour and Welfare Ministry, the average age for men is about 31 and the average age for women is about 29. The government is concerned about this because of the declining birthrate. Japan's population is rapidly graying and there will be fewer younger workers to pay taxes and fund the national pension system as older citizens retire and withdraw pension payments. The country needs more children.

Various factors seem to contribute to the postponing of marriage among Japanese. Social pressure to marry and start a family has definitely declined over the past few decades. A larger percentage of women want to have a career, which means there is less need for them to marry and become dependent on a husband for support. Meanwhile, as a result of the long economic recession, men often do not earn enough to feel comfortable in supporting a family.

若い人たち自身は、本当に結婚したいと思っているのだろうか。各種調査によれば90％が結婚したいと答えたというが、そう答えた18歳から39歳までの回答者のうち半分以上は、**交際相手**または異性の友人がいないらしい。仕事が忙しくて出会いの機会がないという人もいる。こうした人には、**合コン**の新しいスタイルである「**趣味コン**」が使えるかもしれない。趣味を共有する参加者には、異性と出会ったり話をしたりするチャンスができる。夜に皇居の周りをジョギングする趣味コンもあり、男女が二列になって、それぞれ横の人とペアを組んで走る。8分毎に男性列の先頭は最後尾に回り、2番目の男性が先頭に来る。**意気投合**したペアは、お互いをもっとよく知ることができるかもしれないと、イベント終了後の**懇親会**に期待をかけるかもしれない。

自分の中の「理想の相手」の基準に見合う人がいないという独身者もいる。これこそが、**問題の核心**のようである。男性は、自分の母親のように、外で働かず家で**専業主婦**をしてくれる相手を欲しがる。女性は、家事や子育てに協力してくれる男性を求める。どちらの側も、こうした条件を満たす結婚相手を見つけることは難しそうだ。

□ 交際相手 boy / girlfriend
□ 合コン matchmaking party
□ 趣味コン party of like-minded people
□ 意気投合する chemistry is right
□ 懇親会 get-together

□ 問題の核心 crux of the issue
□ 専業主婦 housewife

Do the young people themselves actually want to marry? Surveys show that 90% do, but that more than half of those between 18 and 39 do not have a partner who they might marry or have friends of the opposite sex. Some claim that they are busy with their jobs and do not have opportunities to meet potential partners. A new form of matchmaking party called *shumikon*—named for *shumi* meaning "hobby"— might help them. Participants who share a hobby get a chance to meet and talk with people of the opposite sex. One *shumikon* involves jogging around the Imperial Palace at night in two lines, men in one line, paired with women in another. Every eight minutes, the first man in the line drops back to the end and the second man moves forward. If the chemistry is right, a couple might leave the get-together after the event to get to know each other more.

Others singles claim that they cannot find anyone who matches their standards for an "ideal partner." This seems to be the crux of the issue. Men want partners who are like their own mothers, who were housewives, not working outside the home. Women want partners who will help with the household chores and raising children. Neither side seems able to find a candidate who matches these qualifications.

≫≫ 被害者になる子供たち

　無料のコミュニケーションアプリが、スマートフォンを使う日本の若者の間で大変人気となっている。オンラインの**掲示板アプリ**は、文字や音声で会話をするのに便利である。利用者同士は自分の電話番号やメールアドレスを教えたりする必要がないので、こうしたアプリは**安全**に見える。お互いのID情報さえ知っていればいい。だが最近、**18歳未満**の若い人々にとって、こうしたオンライン掲示板が危険なものとなる可能性があることがわかってきた。

□被害者　victim
□掲示板アプリ　bulletin board app
□安全　safe
□18歳未満　under 18

〉〉〉 Victimizing children

Free communications apps have become very popular among Japanese young people who use smartphones. Online bulletin board apps are convenient for exchanging written messages and voice conversations. The two people using them do not need to give out their own phone number or their email address, so these apps seem safe. All they have to know is each other's ID information. But recently, young people under 18 have found these bulletin boards can be dangerous.

18歳未満でも、こうしたオンライン掲示板上の ID を利用して新しい友だちを作ったり、共通の関心を持った人を探したりすることができる。利用に伴う危険があることもよく考えずに、食事をおごるとか、プレゼントを渡したいとか、あるいは、単に同じ趣味の話をしたいと誘われて、まったく**面識のない人**と不用意に会う約束をしていた子もいた。2013 年上半期に警察が捜査した中で、掲示板上での ID 交換により**児童**が**わいせつ**その他の犯罪被害にあった事件は 117 件あった。こうした被害者の 1/4 は、会う約束をする前、**加害者**に別の意図があるとは疑いもしなかった。彼らは、ネットワーク上で、見知らぬ他人を信用したのだ。

1990 年代、若者の**売春**に新しい形態が現れた。**婉曲的に**「**援助交際**」と呼ばれ、10 代の少女が大人の男性に性的なサービスを提供するとされた。携帯やオンライン掲示板が、これをさらに容易にしてきた。こうした交際は**匿名で**約束が交わされるので、完全に防止することは難しい。

□面識のない人 stranger
□上半期 first half of ~
□児童 minor
□わいせつ sexual attack
□加害者 victimizer

□売春 prostitution
□婉曲的に euphemistically
□援助交際 paid dating
□匿名で anonymously

Minors under 18 can use their ID on these online boards to make new friends or to look for people with common interests. Without considering the potential dangers involved, some young people have casually agreed to meet complete strangers who offer meals or presents, or to simply talk about shared interests. In the first half of 2013, the Japanese police have investigated 117 cases in which minors fell victim to sexual attack or other crimes after exchanging their IDs on such a bulletin board. A quarter of these young people never even questioned the intentions of the victimizer before arranging a meeting. Online they put their trust in a complete stranger.

In the 1990s a new sort of youth prostitution emerged. Euphemistically called "paid dating," teenage girls were said to offer sexual services to adult men. Cell phones and online bulletin boards have made this even easier. Participation in these relationships can be arranged anonymously and it is virtually impossible to prevent them.

>>> 暴力団撲滅

　　日本の企業は、組織犯罪との結びつきを断つのに苦労しているようである。これを思い出させる最近の出来事は、みずほ銀行が系列の信販会社オリエントコーポレーションを通じて、暴力団（ヤクザ）に融資したことが発覚し、問題になった事件である。みずほ銀行は 2010 年に、自動車や電気製品代として総額 2 億円に上る、およそ 228 件の暴力団絡みの融資が実行されていた事実を掴んだ。だが、2013 年にその融資が明るみに出るまで、見て見ぬふりをしていた。銀行幹部は、何年も前から借り手の身元に気付いていたにも関わらず、手をこまねいていたのである。その後、他の大手銀行も似たような融資があることを認めた。

□ 暴力団 organized crime group
□ 撲滅 stamping out
□ 組織犯罪 organized crime
□ 信販会社 credit firm
□ 融資する make a loan

□ 幹部 executive
□ 身元 identity
□ 手をこまねいて fail to do anything

>>> Stamping out organized crime groups

Japanese companies seem to have a hard time breaking off ties with organized crime. A recent reminder of this is the scandal that broke when it was discovered that Mizuho Bank made loans to yakuza through its group credit firm Orient Corporation. The bank discovered in 2010 that some 228 gang-linked loans for automobiles and electronics totaling ¥200 million had been issued. But the bank turned a blind eye to the loans until they came to light in 2013. The bank's executives had been aware of the identity of the borrowers for years but failed to do anything. Other large banks subsequently confessed to making similar loans.

社会 しゃかい

Society

日本の法律は昔から、ゆすり屋、詐欺師、暴力団など「反社会的勢力」との取引に対して生温い。暴力団組織が構える事務所は、地域の公安委員会に登録されている。組員になること自体は犯罪ではない。2007年になって初めて、国はそうした個人や集団との関係を遮断するように企業の「背中を後押しする」指針を出した。全国銀行協会と都道府県もこれに倣い、民間企業による暴力団取引の排除を図った。だが、こうした指針や条例、規則の文言はたいてい曖昧なことが多い。さらにまずいのは、そうした関係を続ける銀行や企業に対し、何ら罰則が設けられていないことである。

□ ゆすり屋 racketeer
□ 詐欺師 fraudster
□ 反社会的勢力 anti-social element
□ 生温い regard leniently
□ 公安委員会 public-safety commission
□ 背中を後押しする encourage
□ 指針や条例 guideline and ordinance
□ 曖昧な vague

Japanese law has long been lenient regarding business dealings with "anti-social elements," a term which includes racketeers, fraudsters and gangsters. Crime syndicates have offices registered with local public-safety commissions. Membership in one is not a crime. It was not until 2007 that the government issued guidelines "encouraging" businesses to cut their links with such individuals and groups. Japan's banking association and prefectural governments followed suit by trying to prevent private businesses from doing business with gangsters. Yet the wording of these guidelines, ordinances and rules is usually vague. Worse yet, there are no penalties for banks or other businesses that continue such ties.

社会 しゃかい

Society

暴力団は、相変わらずみかじめ料を飲食店などに要求したり、強要や恐喝によるビジネスに従事したりと活発に活動している。今も市民は報復を恐れ、そうした活動を通報できない。だが新たな進展も見られる。新しくできた法律は、特定の区域内における暴力団事務所の開設防止にある程度成果を上げている。自分たちの建物や地域から暴力団の立ち退きを求める訴訟を起こそうと、市民団体も形成されている。法律、警察、市民団体が暴力団の影響を減らすことができるのか、現段階では何ともいえない。

□みかじめ料 protection money
□強要や恐喝 coercion and intimidation
□報復 reprisal
□立ち退きを求める evict
□何ともいえない remain to be seen

Yakuza are still active in demanding protection money, especially from bars and restaurants, and engaging in business through coercion and intimidation. Citizens continue to be afraid to report such activities due to fear of reprisals. Some progress is being made. New laws are having some success in preventing gangsters from opening offices in certain areas. Citizen groups have sued to have gangster groups evicted from their buildings and neighborhoods. Whether the laws, the police and citizen groups can reduce yakuza influence remains to be seen.

社会 しゃかい

Society

>>> オレオレ詐欺

　数年前、日本の犯罪者たちは新手の詐欺を思いついた。たとえば息子や孫を騙り、どうしても金が入用な様子で老人に電話をかける。電話の主が使った作り話には、交通事故を起こしたので金を払わないといけない、会社から無断で借りた金を返さないといけないといった例があった。電話を受け取った方は、あまりに気が動転して相手の声にまで気が回らないのだろう。とっさに「息子」または「孫」の用意した口座にお金を振り込まなければと思ってしまう。

　こうした詐欺に対し、繰り返し注意喚起がなされているにも関わらず、犯罪者たちは今なお成功を収めている。あるケースでは、息子を装った電話の主が、会社から「借りた」金を返さないといけないので助けてほしいと60歳代の女性に泣きついた。説得された女性は愛知から東京まで上京し、品川駅近くの路上で「息子の代理」に750万円を手渡した。

□詐欺　fraud
□騙る　pretend to be someone
□気が動転する　be distressed
□気が回らない　can not notice
□注意喚起　warning

□泣きつく　ask in tears
□代理　deputy

>>> "It's me, it's me" frauds

Several years ago Japanese criminals came up with a new variety of fraud. They would call older Japanese pretending to be a son or grandson in desperate need of money. The stories the caller used included having to pay money for a car accident he had caused or to repay money he had borrowed from his company without permission. The person receiving the call would be distressed enough to not notice the caller's voice. That person's first instinct would be to transfer money to the account that the "son" or "grandson" provided.

Despite repeated warnings about such frauds, criminals continue to be successful. In one case, the caller pretending to be a son called a woman in her 60s asking for help in returning money he had "borrowed" from his company. He convinced her to travel from Aichi to Tokyo and hand over ¥7.5 million to "a deputy for the son" on a street near Shinagawa Station.

偽の株や証券、あるいは実際に存在しない商品を勧める電話やパンフレットを使った方法も増えている。また別の手口には、架空の請求書の支払いを要求する電話もある。

警察がこうした事件の中の誰か一人を捕まえたとしても、だいたいは詐欺グループの末端のメンバーである。被害者から現金を回収するだけの役割に過ぎない。首謀者が捕まることはめったにないのである。

□株や証券　stock and bond
□架空の　non-existent
□末端の　low-level
□首謀者　ringleader

Also increasing are the use of phone calls and pamphlets offering fraudulent stocks and bonds or non-existent products. Another pattern is a phone call demanding payment for a non-existent bill.

If police arrest someone in one of these cases, it is usually a low-level member of the group of fraudsters. Their role is simply to collect the cash from the victims. The ringleaders are rarely arrested.

>>> 北朝鮮拉致問題

社会
しゃかい
Society

　1977年、当時13歳だった横田めぐみさんは、日本海の海岸沿いを下校途中に誘拐された。北朝鮮の工作員が、めぐみさんを船に引きずり込み朝鮮半島に連れ去ったのだ。1970年代後半から1980年代初頭にかけて、**少なくとも17名の若い日本人が同じ海岸から北朝鮮人の手で拉致された。これらの拉致被害者らが北朝鮮に連れ去られたのは、北朝鮮スパイに日本語や日本人らしい立ち居振る舞いを教えるためである。

　横田めぐみさんの両親、滋さんと早紀江さんは、他の被害者家族らとともに拉致にあった**肉親**の帰国を求める運動を展開してきた。横田夫妻は、めぐみさんが同じく拉致被害者である韓国人男性と結婚したことを知っている。自分たちには北朝鮮に暮らす孫娘がいることも。めぐみさんが今も**生存**していて、日本に帰国できることを夫妻は願っている。

□拉致 abduction
□工作員 agent
□少なくとも at least
□立ち居振る舞い mannerism
□肉親 relative

□生存 alive

106

>>> North Korean abductions

In 1977, Megumi Yokota, age 13, was kidnapped as she walked home from school along the coast of the Sea of Japan. Agents from North Korea dragged her to their boat and took her to Korea. Between the late 1970s and the early 1980s North Koreans abducted at least 17 young Japanese along the same coast. These abductees were taken to North Korea to teach Japanese language and mannerisms to North Korean spies.

Megumi's parents, Shigeru and Sakie Yokota, have campaigned with other victims' families for the return of their kidnapped relatives. The Yokotas know that Megumi married a South Korean man who was also kidnapped. They know that they have a granddaughter, who lives in North Korea. They hope that Megumi is still alive and may come home to Japan.

多くの日本人は、拉致の噂を単なる**陰謀論**だと思っていた。しかし、2002年に故金正日**総書記**は、北朝鮮が相当数の日本人を拉致してきたこと認めた。だが北朝鮮はこれまで拉致被害者一人一人の**安否**について、信頼できる**証拠**を提示してはいない。北朝鮮の主張は、これら被害者らが死亡しているという。しかし、横田夫妻や多くの支援者たちは、被害者らが今も生存し、日本に返されるべきだと考えている。

被害者に関する情報を提供することで、北朝鮮は日本や米国に対し何かしらの**見返り**を要求する可能性がある。日本も米国も、被害者に何が起きたのかを知ることは望みつつも、そのために北朝鮮に利益を供与するつもりは**毛頭ない**。そんな中、日本の**右翼団体**はこの問題を**在日朝鮮人**批判に利用している。

□ 陰謀論 conspiracy theory
□ 総書記 general secretary
□ 安否 fate, safety
□ 証拠 evidence
□ 見返り reward

□ 毛頭ない not willing to ~ at all
□ 右翼団体 right-wing group
□ 在日朝鮮人 Japan's own Korean population

Many Japanese thought the rumors of kidnappings were simply a conspiracy theory. But in 2002, the late Kim Jong Il admitted that North Korea had abducted a number of Japanese. North Korea has not, however, provided dependable evidence concerning the fate of each of these abductees. It says that the victims are dead. But the Yokotas and many supporters believe the victims are still alive and should be returned to Japan.

To provide any information about the victims, North Korea would demand some kind of reward, from Japan or the United States. The latter countries want to know what happened to the victims, but are not willing to give any benefit to the North Korean government to achieve that. Meanwhile, Japanese right-wing groups use the issue to criticize Japan's own Korean population.

2006年4月28日、当時のアメリカ大統領ジョージ・W・ブッシュと会談する横田早紀江さん
Sakie Yokota meets with U.S. President George W. Bush at the White House in April 2006

>>> 捕鯨をめぐる戦い

　捕鯨をめぐり、日本、ノルウェーおよびアイスランドは多くの反捕鯨国や国際世論を敵に回している。国際捕鯨委員会 (IWC) の規制により、1986 年以降商業捕鯨を行うことは違反とされている。だが IWC 加盟国は、「科学調査」が目的であればクジラの命を奪うことが認められている。日本は IWC 加盟国であり、日本の捕鯨産業は調査目的で何百頭もの鯨の命を奪い続けている。日本は、こうした調査が乱獲から鯨類資源が回復しているかを見極めるために必要であると説明している。また、自国の捕鯨が、いかなる種の生存も脅かすものではないとも言っている。そうではあっても、調査捕鯨で捕獲された鯨の肉は合法的に売ることができる。

□捕鯨 whaling
□国際世論 global public opinion
□敵に回す oppose against
□規制 regulation
□乱獲 over-hunting

□合法的に legally

>>> The battle over whaling

The conflict over whaling pits Japan, Norway and Iceland against dozens of nations that oppose whaling, not to mention global public opinion. Under the regulations of the International Whaling Commission (IWC), since 1986 commercial whaling has been illegal. Countries that belong to the IWC are, however, allowed to kill whales for "scientific research." Japan is a member of the IWC and its whaling industry has continued to kill hundreds of whales for research purposes. Japan says this research is necessary to establish whether whale stocks are recovering from over-hunting. The government says that its whaling is not a threat to the survival of any species. Meanwhile, the meat of whales caught for scientific purposes can be sold legally.

社会 しゃかい
Society

日本の捕鯨賛成派は、捕鯨が長い**文化的伝統**の一部だと主張する。日本の太地町という漁村では小型漁船を使った沿岸捕鯨が行われてきたが、これこそが伝統である。**遠洋**での産業捕鯨が発展したのは、第二次世界大戦後に過ぎない。賛成派はまた、鯨肉が日本の食事の伝統的な一部をなすと主張するが、鯨肉の需要は過去最低である。捕鯨産業が生み出す雇用についての指摘もあるが、直接関連のある**働き口**は非常に少ない。しかも、日本の捕鯨産業は**補助金漬け**である。

捕鯨を批判する人々は、このような「調査」に明確な目的がないと主張する。この立場からすれば、海洋の**生態系**において重要な役割を果たしている鯨を捕ることは愚かな行為といえる。捕鯨産業に依存する働き口がきわめて少なく、しかも補助金を受けているのは儲からないからであるとも指摘する。さらに国際政治の面で見ても、捕鯨は日本のイメージを悪くしている。

いずれの見解も**一理ある**。だが、双方が受け入れ可能な**妥協点**を見つけるのは**容易ではない**。

□ 文化的伝統　cultural tradition

□ 遠洋　distant ocean

□ 働き口　job

□ 補助金漬け　be heavily subsidized

□ 生態系　ecology

□ 一理ある　have a merit

□ 妥協点　compromise

□ 容易ではない　not easy

Supporters of whaling in Japan say that it is part of a deep cultural tradition. In the Japanese fishing village of Taiji, it is a tradition to use small boats in areas close to shore. Industrial whaling in distant oceans only developed in the post-WWII era. Supporters also say that whale meat is a traditional part of the Japanese diet, but demand for that meat is at an all-time low. Supporters point to the jobs that the industry provides, but very few jobs are actually involved. In fact, Japan's whaling industry is heavily subsidized.

Critics of whaling say that there is no clearly stated goal of such "research." From their point of view, it is unwise to harvest whales since they play an important role in ocean ecology. They point out that very few jobs depend on the industry, and those jobs are subsidized because they are not profitable. Finally, in terms of international politics, whaling tarnishes Japan's image.

Each point of view has its merits. But finding a compromise that would be acceptable to both sides is not easy.

社会 しゃかい

Society

【せいかつ】生活

Daily Life

››› コンビニエンスストア

日本の人口密集は、国内店舗数５万店以上というコンビニエンスストア業界の繁栄に貢献している。都市部では、同じチェーンの店舗が道路を挟んで向かい合っているところもある。

こうした店が提供するサービスや商品たるや驚嘆に値する。コピー、小荷物の発送や受取り、コンサートチケットや長距離バスチケットの購入、地方税や公共料金の支払いも可能である。ある大手チェーンは店舗に化粧品も置いているが、最近では待合室を備えた薬局も導入した。牛乳やパンを買っている間に、処方箋の薬を出してもらうことができるのである。

□ 人口密集 population density
□ 繁栄 thrive
□ 驚嘆に値する astounding
□ 地方税 local tax
□ 公共料金 utility bill

□ 待合室 waiting area
□ 導入する introduce
□ 処方箋 prescription

⟫⟫ Convenience stores

Population density in Japan helps one industry thrive; the country has more than 50,000 convenience stores. In some urban areas, there are stores of the same chain facing each other across the street.

The services and products they offer are astounding. You can make a copy of a document, send a parcel, pick up a parcel, buy a concert ticket, purchase a long-distance bus ticket, and pay local taxes and utility bills. One major franchise offers a supply of cosmetics and has recently introduced a pharmacy with a waiting area. You can have your prescription filled while you pick up a liter of milk and a loaf of bread.

Kuha455405

日本語で「コンビニ」と呼ばれるこうした店は、人口動態の変化に対応してきた。かつては若い男性に重点を置いていたが、今は高齢者や料理をする時間がない働く女性たちをターゲットにしている。単身世帯の増加に合わせ、コンビニはさまざまな少量・小分け商品を売り出し、大型スーパーと張り合っている。ポテトサラダや一人前の焼き魚といった一回分の惣菜は、温めればすぐ食べられる。その他の商品の中には健康志向のものもあり、たとえば低カロリーのパン、レタス半玉といった新鮮な野菜、普通は1パック10個入りのところ4個入パックの卵などがある。

　対ファーストフードチェーンとの競争も戦略の柱だ。今では、割とおいしい紙カップ入りのホットコーヒーや、温かい焼き菓子類、フライドチキンを買える店もある。多くの店が、持ち帰りのできるお弁当を各種取り揃えており、レジで頼めば電子レンジで温めてもくれる。コンビニは一ヵ所で何でもそろうパラダイスである。

□ 重点を置く dependent on

□ 単身世帯 single-individual household

□ 少量・小分け商品 small portion product

□ 張り合って compete with

□ 惣菜 delicatessen

□ 健康志向 health-oriented

□ 戦略 tactic

□ 柱 mainstay

Konbini, as they are called in Japanese, have responded to changing demographics. Once dependent on young males, they are now targeting elderly people and working women who do not have time to cook. As the number of single-individual households increase, these stores are competing with large supermarkets by selling small portions of various products. Single-serving deli items, such as potato salad and a single portion of grilled fish, can be eaten right after heating. Among other offerings are health-oriented items, such as low-calorie bread, fresh vegetables like half of a head of lettuce and a pack of four fresh eggs instead of the normal ten.

Competing with fast-food chains is another tactic. You can now buy a reasonably good cup of hot coffee, a warm pastry, and pieces of fried chicken at some stores. Most stores have an assortment of take-out boxed lunches that they will microwave for you at the register. The convenience store is a one-stop paradise.

生活（せいかつ）

Daily Life

≫≫ 自動販売機

　日本の自動販売機は、冷たい飲み物だけでなく温かい飲み物も売っている。コーヒーが飲みたいと思ったら――それもカップで――ボタンを押せば砂糖やミルクを入れることもできるし、ブラックで楽しむこともできる。しかし、日本の自動販売機は、飲み物や袋菓子の次元をはるかに超えている。

　それは「自販機」と呼ばれていて、おみくじ、書籍、レンタルDVD、傘、釣の餌、麺類、アイスクリーム、米、卵、カットりんご、バナナ、ドーナッツ、カレールーまで売っているのである。パーティーに出かける途中に立ち寄って、花束を買うことも可能である。つい最近も日本の下着メーカーが、サイズ表のついた、カラーも豊富なブラジャー自販機を開発したばかりである。

□自動販売機　vending machine
□次元をはるかに超えている　go beyond
　by far
□おみくじ　written oracle
□立ち寄る　stop by

□つい最近　just recently
□下着　lingerie
□豊富な　wide-range

〉〉〉 Vending machines

Japanese vending machines dispense not only cold drinks but hot drinks as well. If you want hot coffee—served in a cup—you push buttons to add sugar and milk, or enjoy it black. But Japanese vending machines go beyond drinks and packaged snacks.

Called *jihanki*, they dispense written oracles, books, DVD rentals, umbrellas, fish bait, noodles, ice cream, rice (uncooked), fresh eggs, sliced apple pieces, bananas, donuts, and packaged curry powder. On your way to a party, you can stop by and pick up a bouquet of flowers from a machine. A Japanese lingerie maker has just developed a bra-dispensing machine, with a size chart and offering a wide-range of colors.

生鮮野菜の自動販売機（東京都北区）
The fresh vegetable vending machine, Kita-ku, Tokyo   *Hisi21*

最新のハイテク自販機には、タッチパネル式画面が付いている。画面の商品は時間帯によって変わり、**内蔵されたセンサー**が利用客の年齢や性別を判断する。そして、その人に合った商品をお勧めするのである。現金だけでなく電子マネーに対応する機械も増えている。

　特に旅行者の間では、無料 Wi-Fi を提供する新しい自販機が客足を集めている。周りに何もない場所でインターネットをチェックしたいと思ったときには、ありがたいサービスである。

　2011年の東日本大震災の後、高機能の新しい自動販売機が開発されてきた。災害発生時に無料で飲料を提供する機能が付いているものもある。また、ある機能は電子表示板に**緊急速報**を表示する。こうした販売機には**予備バッテリー**も**搭載**されている。災害発生時に販売機前の状況を撮影した映像を送るための、カメラ付き自動販売機も開発されている。**通信回線**を介して映像を送り、さらにその場所に向けた緊急情報を表示するのだろう。

□ ハイテク high-tech

□ 内蔵された built-in

□ 緊急速報 emergency bulletin

□ 予備バッテリー battery for backup

□ 搭載する equip

□ 通信回線 telecommunication line

The newest high-tech machines have touch-panel displays. The products on display change with the time of day, and sensors behind the panel estimate the user's age and gender. It then suggests products for that person. Increasingly vending machines accept electronic money as well as cash.

Among travelers especially, a new vending machine draws customers by offering free Wi-Fi. It's a great service when you want to check the Internet in the middle of nowhere.

Following the Great East Japan Earthquake in 2011, new sophisticated vending machines have been developed. One function provides beverages free of charge when a disaster strikes. Another displays emergency bulletins on the electronic display panel. These machines are also equipped with batteries for backup. Camera-equipped vending machines are also being developed to send images of the situation in front of the machine when a disaster strikes. The machine would send the images via a telecommunication line, then display emergency information for that location.

生活 せいかつ

Daily Life

原発

【げんぱつ】

Nuclear Power

⋙ 原子力

原子力は、日本で常に論争の的となってきた。だが日本には代替エネルギーがほとんどない。石油と天然ガスを輸入するか、原子力発電所に依存するかである。だがそれも2011年3月の後あっけなく変わり、2012年5月、日本は1970年以来初めて原発ゼロとなった。すべての原子炉50基が停止されたのである。それでも電力は、天然ガス・石炭・石油火力発電所から供給されていた。国民や企業も省エネを行った。需要ピークの夏場でさえ、停電にはならなかった

福島の炉心溶融事故以来、日本国民の2/3近くが再び原子力に依存することに反対してきている。原発再稼働反対派の意見には、主に3つの論点がある。一つ目は、国民の安全についての不安である。原子力産業は、運用の透明性、安全基準を満たすこと、事故が起きたときの迅速な情報提供において評価が低い。相次ぐ事故は「原子力の安全」が神話であることを明らかにしてきた。

□ 代替エネルギー alternative sources of power
□ ほとんどない have few
□ あっけなく quickly, easily
□ 原子炉 nuclear reactor

□ 炉心溶融事故 meltdown
□ 透明性 transparency
□ 神話 myth

>>> Nuclear power

Nuclear power has always been a contentious issue. Japan has few alternative sources of power. Either it imports oil and natural gas, or it depends on nuclear power plants. But that changed quickly after March 2011, and in May 2012, Japan became nuclear free for the first time since 1970. All 50 nuclear reactors were shut down. Electric power continued to flow through the power grid, from natural gas, coal, and oil-fired thermal power plants. In addition, the public and businesses conserved energy. Even in the summer months of peak demand, there were no brownouts.

Since the Fukushima meltdown, nearly two-thirds of the Japanese public have opposed renewing dependence on nuclear power. There are three central arguments against restarting any of the reactors. One is the concern for public safety. The nuclear industry has a poor track record when it comes to transparency in its operations, meeting safety standards, and speedily providing information when an accident has occurred. Repeated accidents have shown that "nuclear safety" is a myth.

二つ目は、原子力の実際のコストが**世間の目**から隠されていることである。国と東京電力は、原子力を使えば電気代はキロワット時当たり5〜7円になるという。しかし安全対策、**除染費用、廃炉費用、使用済み核燃料棒**の保管、被災者の補償の分を上乗せすると、キロワット時当たり15円にもなる可能性がある。

三つ目は、**核廃棄物**の保管場所である。2013年秋、以前は原発推進派だった小泉元首相が、この問題について思いもよらぬ発言をした。自身の転向理由を説明する中で、小泉元首相は、核廃棄物処理が解決し得ない課題であることを指摘した。原発再稼働は、小泉元首相の言葉を借りれば、核のごみを増やすだけであり、日本には安全性が実証された処理方法がない。

しかし、安倍首相や東京電力、多くの企業、そして住民の雇用確保が必要な自治体は原子炉の運転再開に**意欲的**である。この問題をめぐる議論は長くかかるだろうが、日本の将来にとってきわめて重要となるだろう。

□世間の目　public view

□除染費用　decontamination cost

□廃炉費用　decommissioning expense

□使用済み核燃料棒　spent fuel rod

□核廃棄物　nuclear waste

□意欲的　be eager to

The second is that the actual costs of nuclear power are hidden from public view. The government and the Tokyo Electric Power Company (TEPCO) claim that with the use of nuclear power plants, electricity costs ¥5–7 per kilowatt-hour. However, safety measures, decontamination costs, decommissioning expenses, storage of spent fuel rods, and compensation to people affected by accidents could raise that cost to as much as ¥15 per kilowatt-hour.

The third concerns where to put nuclear waste. In the autumn of 2013, former Prime Minister Koizumi, who once promoted nuclear power, unexpectedly spoke out on this issue. Explaining his change of opinion, he pointed out that the disposal of nuclear waste is an unsolved challenge. Restarting the reactors, he said, would only increase nuclear waste, and Japan has no proven safe way to deal with that waste.

Prime Minister Abe, TEPCO, and many businesses and local governments needing jobs for their citizens, however, are eager to restart the reactors. The debate on this issue will be long and extremely important for Japan's future.

原発

Nuclear Power

柏崎刈羽原子力発電所
Kashiwazaki-Kariwa Nuclear Power Plant

>>> 日本の核廃棄物の行方

原発 *Nuclear Power*

損傷した福島の原子力発電所から出る核物質とは、燃料棒と大量の汚染水である。燃料棒は比較的安全な施設へ移され始めたところである。だがそれも、危険であることには変わりない。施設内の汚染水は二つの場所にある。一つは、大量の一時貯蔵タンク群、もう一つは、施設周辺の土壌である。貯蔵されている方の汚染水は、台風や地震、雷による被害を受ける可能性がある。土壌に浸みこんだ汚染水は、地下水に混入し太平洋に流れ込んでいる。およそ300トンの汚染水が毎日、海に達していると推定される。これらの廃棄物はマスコミが大々的に取り上げているが、他の核廃棄物の方がもしかしたらもっと恐ろしいかもしれない。

全国の原子力発電所50基は2013年秋時点ですべて運転を停止しているが、どの施設も高濃度の放射性物質を抱えており、どこかしらに保管される必要がある。当然のことながら、高レベル核廃棄物処理施設の建設用地の確保は困難である。国民は、そのような施設がすぐ近所にあってほしいとは思わない。

□汚染水 contaminated water
□一時貯蔵タンク temporary storage tank
□土壌 ground
□廃棄物 waste
□大々的に headline-making

□放射性物質 radioactive material
□どこかしらに somewhere

>>> Where does Japan's nuclear waste go?

The nuclear material from Fukushima's damaged nuclear power plant consists of nuclear fuel cells and enormous quantities of contaminated water. The fuel cells are just beginning to be transferred to comparatively safer facilities. They are still dangerous. Contaminated water in the facility is in two places. One is an enormous collection of temporary storage tanks; the other is the ground around the facility. The water that is stored is subject to typhoons, earthquakes, and lightning strikes. The water that has seeped into the ground is flowing into groundwater and the Pacific Ocean. It is estimated that some 300 tons of toxic water reaches the ocean every day. These wastes draw the most headlines, but other nuclear waste is perhaps more frightening.

All of Japan's 50 nuclear power plants remained shut down in the autumn of 2013, but each facility has highly radioactive material that must be kept somewhere. Not surprisingly, suitable locations for building high-level radioactive waste disposal facilities are hard to find. The public is not willing to have such facilities in their immediate neighborhood.

原発 げんぱつ

Nuclear Power

>>> 東京電力

2011年3月11日以前、東京電力株式会社(東電)には、ある評判がすでにあった。東電は、**政界、産業界**に大きな力を持っていたが、安全報告書の**改ざん、違反隠ぺい**、事故隠しでも知られていたのである。

政府規制当局も**共犯**であった。東電を監督するどころか、隠ぺい工作と東電の評判を守ることに手を貸していた。

地震の津波による福島の原子力事故を受けて、東電の評判は**著**しく傷ついた。東電の責任者らは**再三にわたり**情報を公表しなかったという。故障した福島第一原発原子炉を冷却するために海水を注入することを**躊躇**したのは、自社が投資した設備に損害を与えたくなかったからである。

防災対策が不十分だったことを批判されると、福島の災害は「想定外」な出来事によるものと主張した。

□ 政界 politics

□ 産業界 industry

□ 改ざん falsifying

□ 違反隠ぺい covering up violation

□ 共犯 partner in guilt

□ 著しく seriously

□ 再三にわたり time and again

□ 躊躇する hesitate

□ 防災対策 safety measure

>>> Tokyo Electric Power Company

Prior to March 11, 2011, TEPCO already had a mixed reputation. It was a powerful force in politics and industry, but it was also known for falsifying safety reports, covering up violations and keeping accidents secret.

But government regulators were also guilty. Instead of overseeing TEPCO, they participated in cover-ups and in protecting TEPCO.

Following the nuclear disaster at Fukushima resulting from the earthquake and tsunami, TEPCO's reputation was seriously damaged. Its managers reportedly withheld information from the public time and again. It hesitated to cool the crippled Fukushima Daiichi reactors with seawater because it did not want to damage its capital investment.

When criticized for its insufficient safety measures for potential disasters, it claimed that the Fukushima disaster was due to events that were *soteigai*, or "beyond anyone's imagination."

初期の災害は、低レベルの広域汚染を残し何万人にのぼる**強制避難者**を出したが、それだけでなく、福島の原発が制御下に置かれるようになるには数年どころか十数年かかることが明らかになった。原子炉の冷却に使われた汚染水は、**やむを得ず**タンクに保管された——それも結局は漏れた。そしてタンクの数は日ごとに増えた。長期にわたる汚染水対応計画など誰の頭にもなかった。

2013年8月になって東電は、故障した原子力発電所周辺における放射能を帯びた地下水量を低減する計画を発表した。発表は、放射能汚染水が太平洋に流出していたことを**裏付けた**。また、東電が計画に**国費**投入を要請していたことがわかった。

この状況に対処するには、政府が**介入せざるをえない**ことが次第に明らかになった。東電では、家や**生計手段**を失った人々に対する補償を払いきれない。事故がもたらす長期的な被害に対し、効果的な対策も取れなかった。東電は**救済**が必要となるだろうし、納税者に費用負担が求められることになるのだろう。東電は国内の他の原子炉の運転再開を要請したが冗談でやっているわけではなさそうだ。

□ 強制避難者 forced evacuee
□ やむを得ず have no choice but to
□ 裏付ける confirm
□ 国費 government expense
□ 介入する step in to deal

□ ～せざるをえない have no other choice
□ 生計手段 livelihood
□ 救済 help

原発 *Nuclear Power*

In addition to the initial disaster, which left a wide area with low-level contamination and forced tens of thousands of evacuees, it became clear that it would take not years but decades to get the Fukushima plant under control. Radioactive water, used to cool the reactors, had to be stored in tanks—which eventually leaked. And the number of those tanks increased day by day. No one had a plan for dealing with the water in the long term.

Then, in August 2013, TEPCO announced it planned to try to reduce radioactive groundwater at the damaged nuclear plant. This announcement confirmed that radioactive water was leaking into the Pacific Ocean. It also showed that TEPCO was asking for the government to help pay for the project.

Gradually it became apparent that the government would have to step in to deal with the situation. TEPCO would not be able to pay for compensation to those who had lost their homes and livelihood. It could not effectively control the damage that continued to be caused by the disaster. It would need help, and the taxpayers would be called on to pay. TEPCO seemed to see no irony in its call to restart reactors in other parts of the country.

【ぶんか】文化

Culture

>>> 「おもてなし」——日本的ホスピタリティ

文化
ぶんか
Culture

昔から日本人は、親切で他人に思いやりがあるという評判がある。しかし、「おもてなし」という言葉がマスコミにもてはやされる流行語となったのは、2020年の東京五輪招致に向けた最後の一押しというスピーチで使われてからである。五輪招致大使である滝川クリステルが、国際オリンピック委員会 (IOC) の委員たちを前に行ったスピーチの中で、この言葉を使用した。彼女はこの聞きなれない日本語をスピーチの冒頭に持ってきて、「お・も・て・な・し」と、一音一音区切って発音した。それから、お辞儀とともにこの言葉を繰り返した。マスコミの中にはこのスピーチを笑いのネタにした人もいたが、一般の人々の反応は肯定的であった。五輪開催までの何年間かは、この言葉が何度も繰り返されるだろうし、多くの別の目的に使われることは間違いない。

☐ おもてなし hospitality
☐ 流行語 buzzword
☐ 五輪招致大使 Olympic bid ambassador
☐ 冒頭に at the beginning
☐ 一音 syllable

☐ 笑いのネタにする make fun of
☐ 肯定的 positive
☐ 間違いない undoubtedly

>>> *"Omotenashi"*: Japanese hospitality

Japanese have long had a reputation for being kind and considerate of others. But the term *omotenashi* did not become a media buzzword until it was used in a speech during the final push to bring the 2020 Olympic Games to Tokyo. Olympic bid ambassador Christel Takigawa used the word in her speech before the International Olympic Committee (IOC). She began her speech with this unusual Japanese word, pronounced one syllable at a time *o-mo-te-na-shi*. She then repeated it with a bow. Some people joked about the speech in the media, but the response from the general public was positive. The word will be repeated in the years leading up to the Olympics and will undoubtedly be used for many different purposes.

文化

Culture

「おもてなし」とはホスピタリティのことであり、思いやり、そして相手にやすらぎや居場所という恩恵を与えるといったニュアンスを持つ。伝統的な日本の旅館なら、温かい歓迎や接客とでもいえばいいのだろう。個人の家庭だったら、主人が客人にどう心を砕くかといったことになろう。

□思いやり nuance of politeness
□やすらぎ peace
□居場所 space
□恩恵 benefit
□心を砕く take care of

Omotenashi means "hospitality," and it carries the nuance of politeness and giving the other person the benefit of space and peace. In a traditional Japanese inn, it would refer to the warm reception and treatment of a guest. In a private home, it would refer to how a host takes care of a welcome visitor.

文化 *Culture*

>>> 和食

　和食すなわち伝統的な日本料理が、ユネスコの無形文化遺産に登録された。フランス料理、地中海料理(スペイン、ギリシャ、イタリアおよびモロッコ)、メキシコ料理、ケシケキ(トルコ)に続く5番目の食文化として和食が加えられる。

　和食には重要な特徴がいくつかあるが、第一に米、野菜、味噌、醤油、酒といった食材を基本としていることがほとんどである。第二に、この伝統的料理が、南北に長い日本列島に沿って、北から南へと大きく異なっている。京都の九条葱のような食材は、日本列島の限られた地域でしか栽培されていなかったり、数週間あるいは数ヵ月の間しか出回らなかったりする。和食はこうした季節の食材を利用しており、正月、田植え、稲刈りといった年中行事と関連するその土地の風習と結びつきがあることが多い。

□無形文化遺産 intangible cultural heritage

□伝統的料理 traditional cuisine

□栽培する grow

□出回らない not to be marketed

□正月 New Year's holidays

□田植え rice planting

□稲刈り harvesting

□土地の風習 local social custom

>>> *Washoku*

Washoku, traditional Japanese cuisine, has been registered as a UNESCO intangible cultural heritage. It joins French, Mediterranean (Spain, Greece, Italy and Morocco), Mexican, and Keskek (Turkey) as the fifth such food culture to be listed.

Washoku has several important characteristics, the first of which is that it usually is based on ingredients such as rice, fish, vegetables, miso, shoyu and saké. Second, this traditional cuisine differs from north to south along Japan's long north-south archipelago. Ingredients such as Kyoto's leeks may be grown only in limited areas of the island chain, and may only be in season for a few weeks or months. *Washoku* makes use of these seasonal ingredients and often has a connection with local social customs related to annual events such as the New Year's holidays, rice planting, and the harvesting season.

皮肉なのはこの登録が、日本人の若い世代が和食から離れつつある中にやってきたことである。若い世代は、日本の伝統的な料理屋で出されるような洗練された和食を試す機会も、また、子供の頃から家で母親に教わらない限りは、毎日の食卓に載せるような和食の作り方を学ぶ機会もほとんどないのである。

文化
Culture

□ 皮肉なのは ironically
□ 洗練された elegant
□ 食卓 table

Ironically, this registration comes at a time when younger generations of Japanese are drifting away from *washoku*. They have fewer occasions to try elegant *washoku*, such as that served in Japanese traditional restaurants, and to learn how to prepare everyday *washoku*, unless their mothers taught them at home when they were children.

››› 旨味

　日本語で「旨味」と言えば、良い出汁のことである。それは、旨いという感覚を舌に残し、食べ物のさまざまな味覚を調和させている。すべての味をひとつにまとめるのにも役立っている。

　欧米では長らく、味覚には塩味、酸味、甘味、苦味の四基本味があると信じられていた。フランス料理のシェフ、エスコフィエは、これら四基本味の単純な組合せ以外の味覚を持つ料理を生み出した。彼は料理に仔牛のブイヨン、すなわち旨味の濃縮液を使った。特別な名前は付かなかったが、彼が創り出したものは新しい何かの始まりだった。

□ 出汁　broth
□ 旨い　delicious
□ 味覚　taste
□ 調和させる　balance
□ 濃縮液　concentrated liquid

》》 *Umami*

The Japanese term "umami" is described as a pleasant broth. It leaves a delicious sensation on the tongue and it balances the various tastes of food. It helps to bring all of the flavors together.

In the West, people long believed that there were four primary tastes: salty, sour, sweet and bitter. The French chef Escoffier created meals that included tastes that were not just a combination of these four flavors. He used veal stock, a concentration of umami, in his cooking. There was no special name for it, but his creations were the beginning of something new.

エスコフィエ
Escoffier

東京帝国大学の化学者、池田菊苗も、五番目の味覚があることに気がついた。池田は、その味覚を生み出すものが何なのかを探る研究に着手した。彼は実験を重ね、それがアスパラガス、チーズ、トマト、肉、昆布の中にあることを発見した。1908年、池田はその旨いという味覚が、グルタミン酸によるものであることを突き止めた。池田はそれを新たに「旨味」と名付けたが、今日この名称は広く使われている。

　幸いなことに、旨味の豊富な食材はどの食文化にも存在する。イタリア料理では、きのこ類、トマト、パルメザンチーズ。中華料理なら、ニラや白菜、鳥がらスープ。日本料理では、昆布、椎茸、鰹節である。こうした食材は組み合わせて使った方が、単独で使うよりも旨味は増す。

□着手する　set out
□昆布　kombu seaweed
□名称　name
□幸いなことに　fortunately
□鰹節　dried bonito flake

□組み合わせる　mix
□単独で　one alone

Kikunae Ikeda, a chemist at Tokyo Imperial University, also sensed that there was a fifth taste. Ikeda set out to discover what created that taste. Through his experiments, he found it in asparagus, cheese, tomatoes, meat and *kombu* seaweed. In 1908 he discovered that the delicious taste was created by glutamic acid. He renamed it "umami," the name that is universally used today.

Fortunately, every food culture has ingredients that are rich in umami. Italians have it in mushrooms, tomatoes and Parmesan cheese. Chinese have it in Chinese leeks, cabbage and chicken soup. Japanese have it in *kombu* seaweed, shiitake mushrooms, and dried bonito flakes. Umami makes the taste of these mixed ingredients better than the taste of each one alone.

>>> 職人

日本の伝統的な技術者はその数が減っており、**跡を継ごう**とする若者はほとんどいない。しかし、国外からの注目度は高まっている。

「職人」として知られるこうした人々は、熟練した技術を持っているだけでなく、それぞれの職業に身を捧げ、必要な技術を習得して、**なし得る限り**最高の品質を生み出したいという熱い思いを持っている。職人は、仕事に真剣に取り組み、常に腕を磨く努力をし、**社会的責任**をしっかりと認識して、**克己心**と集中力を維持するものとされている。そして誇りをかけて、見た目に美しく、デザインに優れ、**耐久性**と**使い勝手の良さ**を兼ね揃えた製品を生み出している。かつてはこうした職人たちが国内の至るところに見られ、生活に必要な品々を手作業で作り出していた。安価な**大量生産商品**がこうした職人たちの生計を脅かしてきたが、生き残った職人たちは、その**揺るぎない**意志に惚れるファンを獲得してきている。

□跡を継ぐ follow in someone's footsteps
□なし得る限り possibly
□社会的責任 social responsibility
□克己心 self-discipline
□耐久性 durability

□使い勝手の良さ usability
□大量生産商品 mass-produced goods
□揺るぎない determinate

⟩⟩⟩ *Shokunin*, Japan's artisans and craftspeople

Japanese artisans and craftsmen are declining in numbers, and few young people are prepared to follow in their footsteps. But they are attracting increasing attention outside of Japan.

Known as *shokunin*, these men and women possess not only technical skills but a devotion to their respective trade and a desire to master the necessary skills to produce the best quality possible. The *shokunin* is supposed to take work seriously, constantly aspire to improve, take social responsibilities to heart, and maintain self-discipline and focus. The *shokunin* takes pride in producing products that are aesthetically pleasing, well designed, durable, and easy to use. These artisans were once found throughout the country producing the essential goods of everyday life by hand. Cheaper mass-produced goods have threatened their livelihood, but those who have survived are gaining admirers for their determination.

「町工場」には今も多くの職人が働いており、刃物類、自動車部品、鎚起銅器、台所用品、竹籠など実にさまざまな日用品を作り出している。

別のタイプの職人に、カリスマ左官、挾土 秀平がいる。彼は岐阜県にある自分の会社の仕事を通して、左官としてその名前を知られるようになった。首相官邸の土壁や、2008 年の北海道洞爺湖サミットで使われた土の円卓なども手掛けた。その技術には、温度、湿度、季節の変化、使う材料のちょっとした違いにも敏感であることが求められる。やり直しがきかないため、タイミングやスピードもきわめて重要である。ニューヨークに招かれて個展も開催しており、まさに日本の職人の典型なのである。

□鎚起銅器 hammered copper pot
□竹籠 bamboo basket
□カリスマ charisma
□左官 plasterer
□敏感 sensitivity

□やり直しがきかない no opportunity to do a makeover
□個展 solo exhibition
□典型 epitome

The *machi koba*, small city factories, are where many *shokunin* still work producing knives, auto parts, hammered copper pots, kitchen utensils, bamboo baskets, and a wide variety of other items for daily use.

Another type of *shokunin* is the charismatic plasterer Shuhei Hasado. Through his company in Gifu prefecture, he has made a name for himself as a plasterer. He plastered the clay walls of the Prime Minister's Office and the round clay table used in the G8 summit in Hokkaido in 2008. His skill requires a sensitivity to temperature, humidity, seasonal change and slight differences in the materials he uses. Timing and speed are essential, because there is no opportunity to do a makeover. Invited to hold a solo exhibition of his work in New York, he is the epitome of a Japanese craftsman.

文化 Culture

>>> 富士山と世界遺産

富士山は何世紀にもわたり、聖なる山とされ、日本の象徴と見なされてきた。庶民がこの山に登り始めたのは室町時代 (1336–1575) のことである。江戸時代 (1603–1868) になって、山そのものがありがたい神様として崇拝されるようになった。この山を登ることは魂を清めるための、いわゆる巡礼のようなものなった。

富士山は東京からわずか2時間の距離にあり、首都圏にもアクセスしやすい。海外から訪れる人々の中には、旅行の計画に富士登山を入れる人もいる。かなり以前に五合目付近まで道路が敷かれ登山は楽になった。東京都心から車で来て、車を置いたら、登山を開始できる。あるいは東京からバスに乗って来て、バスの駐車場から登り始めることも可能だ。夥しい数のこうした登山客は、山とその周辺地域に大きな影響を及ぼした。ゴミや大気汚染、交通渋滞は年々増加する一方である。2012年には、およそ32万人の登山者があった。

□庶民 commoner
□崇拝する worship
□巡礼 pilgrimage
□五合目 mountain's fifth station
□道路を敷く construct a road

□夥しい数の huge number of
□交通渋滞 heavy traffic

>>> Mt. Fuji and World Heritage status

Mount Fuji has been considered a sacred mountain and a symbol of Japan for centuries. Commoners began to climb the mountain in the Muromachi period (1336–1573). In the Edo period (1603–1868) the mountain itself came to be worshipped as a benevolent deity. Climbing it became a kind of pilgrimage, a way to purify one's soul.

Mt. Fuji is only two hours from Tokyo, so it is accessible to the largest metropolitan area in the country. Some visitors from abroad include the climb in their travel plans. Climbing became easier long ago when a road was constructed to a point about halfway to the peak. People can drive from downtown Tokyo, park their cars and begin their climb. Or they can travel by bus from Tokyo and start from the bus parking area. This huge number of visitors had a major impact on the mountain and the surrounding area. Trash, air pollution, and heavy traffic have increased year by year. In 2012 some 320,000 people made the climb.

2013年、多くの日本人が富士山のユネスコ世界文化遺産リスト入りを祝った。富士山の新しい肩書きがもたらす影響を心配する人々も、中にはいた。その年の夏、ほとんど何の準備も装備もないような登山客が一気に増加した。富士山は、標高3776m、天気も変わりやすく、山道は岩だらけ、山頂の気温は低い。こうした登山客の中には、防寒対策もなく、登山靴も履かず、水も食料もないに等しく、夜間登山用のヘッドライトさえ持たずに山道に降り立つ人もいた。中には過去に一度も登山をしたことがない人までいた。

富士山へのアクセスを制限することは不可能である。登山にはそこまで特別な装備は要らないが、知識と健康、適切な用具、食料と水、持久力は不可欠である。

□肩書き status
□装備 equipment
□一気に suddenly
□標高 true height
□防寒対策 low-temperature gear

□ないに等しい virtually nought
□持久力 physical endurance

In 2013 many Japanese celebrated when Mt. Fuji was listed as a cultural asset in Unesco's World Heritage list. Some Japanese worried about the impact that the new status would have. During summer that year, visitors with virtually no preparation or equipment suddenly increased. Mt. Fuji is 3,776 meters high, has rapid changes in weather, rocky trails, and low temperatures at the top. Some of these visitors arrived on the trail with no low-temperature gear, no boots, virtually no water or food, and no headlamps for climbing at night. Some had never climbed any mountain before.

It is impossible to restrict access to the mountain. While the climb does not require much special equipment, it does require knowledge, good health, appropriate gear, food and water, and physical endurance.

≫≫ スタートは桜の花とともに

　他の多くの国々と違い、日本では国の**会計年度**が始まるのも、学校や職場で新年度が始まるのも4月1日である。

　数年前、日本の大学で、学校のスタートを9月に変えようという議論がなされた。**狙い**は、他国からの学生が海外で使用されているスケジュールに合わせて学業を開始できるようにすることだった。またそうすることで、日本の学生も欧米の**大学暦**に合わせて**留学**することが**容易**になるだろうとの考えだった。しかし、導入を決めた大学はほとんどなかった。そこで今度は、実際の「スタート」を4月のままとし、**4学期制**を開始しようという議論がなされた。

□会計年度 fiscal year
□狙い intended purpose
□大学暦 academic calendar
□留学する study abroad
□容易に easily

□4学期制 quarter system

>>> Starting with the cherry blossoms

Unlike many other countries, in Japan government starts its fiscal year, schools start their academic year, and companies start employment year on April 1.

Several years ago, Japanese universities discussed changing the start of school to September. The intended purpose would be to allow students from other countries to start their studies on the schedule used abroad. Doing so would also allow Japanese students to more easily take a year abroad matching the Western academic calendar. But few universities decided to do so. Then they discussed initiating a quarter system, but leaving the actual "start" in April.

文化ぶんか

Culture

変更についてさまざまな提案は、どれもなかなか良いアイデアに思われる。しかし、大学だけを変えるのは非現実的である。うまく機能させるためには、人によっては、家庭での生活習慣や会社との雇用契約、休暇の取得時期など社会全体のさまざまな物事のタイミングを変えなくてはならなくなるかもしれない。何の不思議な力も働いていないのに、日本は4月1日スタートに囚われているようだが、その日は文化圏によってはエイプリルフールのところもある。

□非現実的 unrealistic
□雇用契約 hiring contract
□囚われている stuck with
□文化圏 culture area

The various proposals for change seem like good ideas. However, it is unrealistic to change only universities. One would have to change family routines, company hiring, vacation times, and other timings throughout the society in order to make it work. Without some form of miracle, Japan seems stuck with starting on April 1, which in some cultures is April Fools' Day.

>>> 関西VS関東

日本は、地域によって文化が大きく異なる。もっともわかりやすい例は、関東（東京が中心）と関西（大阪が中心）との違いである。西の関西と東の関東の大きな違いが明確なものとなったのは徳川時代（1600–1867）である。東京（当時は江戸）は、国を治める行政官である武士が大多数を占める町となった。江戸の人口の約半分は武家であり、全国から集まって来ていた。一方大阪は、商人が多数派を占め、武士の割合は1％に満たなかった。

おそらく商人という歴史もあってか、関西人は地に足が付いていて、実利を重んじ、社交的で、ユーモアのセンスに長けると見られることが多い。日本でもっとも有名なお笑い芸人の多くが、関西出身である。関東人は反対によそよそしく、生真面目で、都会的だと思われている。関西人からすれば関東人は、人情味に欠け、人生の喜びも知らないように見える。

□ 行政官 ruling administrator
□ 武士 samurai
□ 武家 samurai class
□ 地に足が付いて down-to-earth
□ 実利を重んじる practical

□ 社交的 outgoing
□ お笑い芸人 comedian
□ 人情味 human warmth

>>> Kansai vs. Kanto

文化 ぶんか

Culture

Japan displays a significant amount of cultural diversity. The clearest example of this is the difference between the Kanto region (centered on Tokyo) and Kansai (centered on Osaka). Profound differences between Kansai in the west and Kanto in the east became clear during the Tokugawa period (1600–1867). Tokyo (then called Edo) became a city dominated by the samurai, the ruling administrators of the country. Almost half of Edo's population came from the samurai class, and they gathered from all over the country. In contrast, Osaka was dominated by merchants, with a population of less than 1% samurai.

Perhaps as a result of their history as merchants, the people of Kansai are commonly seen as down-to-earth, practical, outgoing, and possessing a good sense of humor. Many of the most famous comedians of the country come from Kansai. The people of the Kanto region, by contrast, are seen as more reserved, more formal, and more sophisticated. From the Kansai point of view, Kanto people lack human warmth and the joy of life.

こうした違いは薄れつつあるものの、料理にも、ちょっとした名残を見つけることができる。関東では豚肉の方が好まれるが、関西では牛肉の方が好まれるといわれている。うどんなどの麺つゆは、関東より関西の方が薄味である。「お好み焼き」や「たこ焼き」が生まれたのは大阪であり、大阪で食べるのが一番おいしい。

関西気質にぴったりの関西弁は、気取らず、感情豊かで、関東地方の話し方と比べて賑やかだと思われている。関西では、方言は誇りであり、地元の人々は東京で話されている「標準」語をほとんど取り入れようとはしない。関西と関東の対抗意識は、一つには、どちらの地域も相手の地域の慣習やしきたりが自分たちの好みに合わないと思っていることがある。

□ 名残 trace

□ 麺つゆ broth in noodle dish

□ 関西気質 Kansai character

□ 関西弁 Kansai dialect

□ 方言 dialect

□ 標準語 standard dialect

□ 対抗意識 rivalry

□ しきたり custom

The differences are fading, but even in cuisine, we find a few traces of the differences. It is said that pork is preferred in Kanto, while beef is preferred in Kansai. The broth in noodle dishes, such as udon, is lighter in Kansai than in Kanto. Osaka gave birth to *okonomiyaki* and *takoyaki*, and that is the best place to eat it.

Appropriate to Kansai character, the Kansai dialect is seen as more casual, emotional and louder than the dialect spoken in the Kanto area. In Kansai, the dialect is a source of pride and the local people make little attempt to adopt the "standard" dialect spoken in Tokyo. The rivalry between Kansai and Kanto comes, in part, because each region finds the manners and customs of the other region not to their liking.

装　幀＝斉藤　啓　（ブッダプロダクションズ）
英文校閲＝Michael Brase
写　真＝photolibrary.jp, wikipedia, 足成ほか

Furigana JAPAN
日本の論点
Japan Today and How It Got This Way

2017年3月1日　第1刷発行

著　者　ジェームス・M・バーダマン
訳　者　相場　妙

発行者　浦　晋亮
発行所　IBCパブリッシング株式会社
〒162-0804 東京都新宿区中里町29番3号　菱秀神楽坂ビル9F
Tel. 03-3513-4511　Fax. 03-3513-4512
www.ibcpub.co.jp

印刷所　中央精版印刷株式会社

© ジェームス・M・バーダマン 2014
© IBC Publishing, Inc. 2017

Printed in Japan

落丁本・乱丁本は、小社宛にお送りください。送料小社負担にてお取り替えいたします。
本書の無断複写（コピー）は著作権法上での例外を除き禁じられています。

ISBN978-4-7946-0465-1